BUSINESS
*SMARTS*™



# ACCOUNTING MADE EASY

JOHN ALEXANDER

PRICE STERN SLOAN
Los Angeles

**A TERN ENTERPRISES BOOK**



Published by Price Stern Sloan, Inc.
360 North La Cienega Boulevard, Los Angeles, California 90048

Printed in the United States of America
9 8 7 6 5 4 3 2 1



**Library of Congress Cataloging-in-Publication Data**
Alexander, John.
Accounting made easy : Business smarts / John Alexander.
p. cm.
ISBN 0-89586-766-4
1. Accountants--United States. 2. Auditors--United States.
3. Accounting firms--United States. I. Title.
HF5627.A43 1990 89-27734
338.4'7657'0973--dc20 CIP

*Accounting Made Easy*
was prepared and produced by
Tern Enterprises, Inc.
15 West 26th Street
New York, New York 10010

Cover design: Paul Matarazzo
Cover illustration: Donald Richey
Interior design: Lynn Fischer

Box on page 12 is based on salary information provided by
*Accounting Office Management & Administration Report.*

Information for the charts on pages 27, 28 and 93 was provided
by *Bowman's Accounting Report.*

# CONTENTS

# INTRODUCTION

The generic title "accountant" means different things to different people and is virtually impossible to define meaningfully or accurately. This book will try to explain why this is so.

But while the name "accountant" can be applied to a wide variety of individuals, the term "accounting profession" is not only definable but also generally applicable to a specific group of individuals who have been licensed to practice as certified public accountants (CPAs). Although many non-CPAs justifiably call themselves "accountants," it is CPAs who generally come to mind when one refers to the accounting profession or industry. It is predominantly on CPAs that this book is focused.

Accountants are involved in a complex variety of activities in virtually all areas of business and finance. This book attempts to describe the different kinds of accountants and some of the more common jobs they perform. The technical guidelines under which CPAs work are unfathomable to those not intimately familiar with the profession, and it would be sheer folly to attempt to explain them in the space of this book, except in their broadest context. At the same time, many of the applications of these guidelines affect large numbers of people and, where appropriate, attempts have been made to describe some of these situations.

In a broader sense, this book, designed as a short course in the accounting field, shows what a vital service the accounting profession provides to the business and financial communities, demonstrates its importance by illustrating how many people are touched by it on a daily basis and outlines some of the challenges facing accountants as they embark on their second century as a profession in the United States. Most important, *Accounting Made Easy* gives those readers thinking about entering this challenging, diverse profession everything they need to know to get started on the right foot.

Chapter 1

# A BRIEF HISTORY OF ACCOUNTING

Looking over the shoulders of the first Neanderthal entrepreneurs at the primordial dawn of commerce was, to nobody's great surprise, an accountant. As the first acts of trade were negotiated, and as each party to the deal wondered whether the result meant profit or loss, to whom did each participant turn?

Thus has it been down through the ages. As business and finance became more complex, as greater numbers of parties got in on the deals and as business came to be the axle upon which the world turned, so has the accountant become more and more a player. As we approach the twenty-first century, the accountant is a part of literally every business and financial transaction that takes place.

It didn't take very long before accountants had progressed from auditing prehistoric clam shells to providing more sophisticated services for their clients. While the historical record is sketchy, there is evidence that as early as 3000 B.C., some enterprising souls were recording the business deals of the Babylonians and Assyrians in clay ledger books. Likewise, the legendary trading carried out by the seafaring Phoenicians, the refined governing bodies of the ancient Greeks and the military budgets and associated tax collecting of the Romans were all being dutifully recorded by local accountants. Whether they were keeping their records on clay, papyrus or stone the need was there and the job was carried out.

## The Birth of Bookkeeping

It remained for the Renaissance Italians to develop what could be called the first permanent bookkeeping system sometime between the fourteenth and sixteenth centuries. The first historic recording of systematic accounting took place with the publication, in 1494, of *Summa de Arithmetica Geometria Proportioni et Proportionlita,* written by the Franciscan monk Fra Luca Pacioli. This epic was notable because it included the first written description of double-entry bookkeeping.

Since the estimable monk's book conveniently appeared just after the invention of the printing press, the work spread across Europe and was understandably adopted and refined by practitioners of this developing art in other lands.

While all this was going on, governments, at the city or state level, were finding it necessary to keep more detailed records of their burgeoning transactions. Commerce and trade were developing at unprecedented levels, more and more different kinds of taxes were being collected and, most important, vastly larger numbers of people were becoming involved, all of which increased the need for more sophisticated systems to keep track of everything.

While the Italian bookkeepers of the sixteenth century could be said to be the first faint nucleus of what came to be a true profession, little further development took place as far as common systems or techniques until the nineteenth century and the onset of the Industrial Revolution in the British Isles. At that time, a number of new business developments took place that, taken together, lent new importance to the work accountants were doing.

With the Industrial Revolution came speculation. New companies needed to raise capital, so they offered stock. Some of these companies failed, bringing on bankruptcies. Midway through the century, the British Companies Acts were introduced, requiring corporations to report in detail on their financial operations—what in effect were the first annual reports. These reports had to be examined, thus creating the need for the first audits. These new procedures created new jobs for the only people capable of handling them—those who, until then, had been generically labeled "bookkeepers" and who now came to be called with increasing frequency "accountants."

If London was the hub of this evolution of the accounting profession, it fell to the Scots to bring to it some sense of organization. In 1854, a small group of Scottish accountants founded under a royal charter the Society of Accountants in Edinburgh. These latter-day organization men were the first to be designated chartered accountants, the name by which accountants are still designated in the United Kingdom, Canada and most other English-speaking countries except the United States.

Ensuing years saw the founding of numerous local accounting societies, with membership more and more confined to those who practiced the profession of accounting on a full-time basis. Two organizations, the Institute of Accountants, with strict membership requirements, and the Society of Accountants in England, with less stringent membership requirements, competed for members until 1880, when a royal charter brought about the Institute of Chartered Accountants in England and Wales. This organization was founded on carefully delineated standards of conduct, and an examination was required for entry as a member.

## Accounting Comes to America

The professionalizing of accountancy in England and Scotland inevitably led to importation to the United States. The same combination of economic and commercial development that had existed in England at the time of the Industrial Revolution came about in the United States as the nineteenth century drew to a close. Once again, the accountants were there and up to the challenge, although they needed some help in the early stages from their brethren in the United Kingdom.

Actually, the British had ulterior motives in helping develop the accounting profession in the United States. British investors were pouring more and more capital into American industry. Those investors, quite naturally, wanted to know how their investments were doing, and, rather than trust American accountants, the British sent their own. The result was the formation of U.S. branch offices of British accounting firms.

One British accountant, Edwin Guthrie, had a direct hand in the formalization of the accounting profession in the United States. Not only did Guthrie establish the first formal accounting firm on American soil, but he was also directly responsible for the formation of the first accounting association in the United States, the American Association of Public Accountants, in 1887. This group was the original, direct ancestor of today's **American Institute of Certified Public Accountants (AICPA)**.

The American Association of Public Accountants was the leader in seeking legislation to regulate the profession. This law, passed in New York State in 1896, provided for accountants to be certified only after passing a written examination and meeting other requirements related to education and work experience. Those who passed muster became known as **certified public accountants**, or **CPAs**. Other states followed suit, and by 1904 a total of seven states had more or less similar laws on the books. Today, CPAs are still licensed by the states within which they practice, although all fifty-four licensing jurisdictions (the fifty states plus the District of Columbia, Puerto Rico, the Virgin Islands and Guam) make use of the same qualifying test, the **Uniform CPA Examination**.

# A New Era

Through war, depression, the introduction of a personal income-tax system and the growing complexity of government, the profession grew rapidly. But the Great Depression proved the demarcation line between the old and the new era. Prior to that most cataclysmic economic event in the country's history, people had pretty much left accountants alone to do their own thing. After the depression, others started to take an interest, chief among them the federal government. The reason was that the economic downturn had resulted in the failure of a great number of businesses, and people who had invested in these companies had lost money.

The instrument of this change was, first, the Securities Act of 1933, which contained provisions requiring auditors to examine the financial statements of companies registered with, at that time, the Federal Trade Commission. These provisions for the first time imposed upon accounting firms a liability to those who made use of auditors' reports (primarily investors).

Just one year later, Congress passed the Securities Exchange Act of 1934, and also created the Securities and Exchange Commission (SEC) to enforce both acts. This was the law that first required publicly traded companies to file an annual report. The financial statements contained in that report had to bear the opinion of an independent auditor. The Securities Acts also gave the SEC a strong oversight position in that the agency could, if necessary, set accounting principles, the guiding rules under which accountants carried out their work.

Other elements of the profession were also changing dramatically in the years just prior to World War II. New expertise was needed to cope with the relatively new income tax on individuals and corporations. Accountants were also entering into a relationship with the Treasury Department and the tax-writing committees of Congress that would see the profession develop a strong influence on the writing of the tax laws.

The profession began to grow by leaps and bounds, doubling in numbers roughly every ten years. By 1960, the AICPA had almost 38,000 members, by 1970 there were 74,413, by 1980 there were 101,319 and, midway through 1989, membership was approaching 300,000. Rough estimates put that membership at anywhere from two-thirds to three-quarters of all the CPAs in the country.

The years between 1960 and the present brought remarkable growth, a consolidation of accounting standards and the establishment of an independent standard-setting body, the **Financial Accounting Standards Board (FASB)**. During this period, the first questions about the quality of the work done by auditors arose, the liability issue attracted great attention and the profession was pushed into taking unprecedented steps in order to retain its self-regulatory status. At the same time, competition between accounting firms grew fierce, forcing the profession to recognize the necessity of modern-day marketing strategies, including advertising. In fact, the AICPA did not lift its ban on advertising until 1977.

The nature of the once-arch-conservative profession changed quickly in the 1970s and 1980s. Accountants were beginning to wield an influence in almost every area of the business and financial communities that would have been unthinkable just twenty years earlier. Despite some negative headlines in newspapers, accountants enjoyed a reputation in the eyes of the general public and knowledgeable segments of the business community that was the envy of other professions.

# Chapter 2

# WHO OR WHAT IS AN ACCOUNTANT?

A quick telephone inquiry at the Bureau of Labor Statistics in Washington, D.C., will reveal that, at least according to the federal government, there are more than one million accountants currently working in the United States. If this number seems large, at least to the relatively well informed about the profession, there's a simple explanation. In all but twenty-one states, the District of Columbia, Puerto Rico, Guam and the U.S. Virgin Islands, anyone can call himself or herself an accountant. To use the title accountant in Alabama, Alaska, Arkansas, California, Connecticut, Hawaii, Idaho, Indiana, Massachusetts, Nevada, New Jersey, North Dakota, Ohio, Oklahoma, Pennsylvania, Rhode Island, South Carolina, South Dakota, Texas, Utah and West Virginia, an individual must generally be a CPA or a licensed public accountant and must hold a permit to practice and/or maintain a registered office in the state. (The difference between CPAs and licensed public accountants is simple: CPAs have passed the Uniform CPA Examination.)

Quite obviously, many individuals in the other twenty-nine states who might not be thought of as accountants in the strict meaning of the term nevertheless apply it to themselves. At least they do so on their federal income-tax returns, the source of much of the Bureau of Labor Statistics's information. In fact, it seems highly unlikely that these statistics are accurate.

Rather, working with numbers that at least have a degree of statistical accuracy—from the AICPA, state CPA societies and elsewhere—we know that there are between 350,000 and 400,000 certified public accountants in the country. But even the CPAs, with their assumed affinity for numbers, are unable to come up with a precise figure for how many of themselves there are, ostensibly because many of them are licensed to practice in more than one state or jurisdiction. Unfortunately, the **National Association of State Boards of Accountancy (NASBA)** can't account for the overlap, and many are counted more than once.

Like many professions, the CPAs are subdivided, with many serving in areas other than public practice, such as industry, government and education. Not surprisingly, these individuals belong to specialized membership organizations that also count among their respective members others who are not necessarily CPAs. These groups include the **National Association of Accountants (NAA)**, management accountants; the **American Accounting Association (AAA)**, educators; the **Institute of Internal Auditors (IAA)** and the **Financial Executives Institute (FEI)**. There is also an **Association of Government Accountants (AGA)** and a **National Association of Public Accountants (NAPA)**.

Below this grouping of true professionals, there is a category that, while not usually certified or formally organized as a profession, nevertheless includes a significant number of semi-professional practitioners. In this group one can find the thousands of **bookkeepers** who work on a full- or part-time basis in companies of all sizes. We find here as well the equally impressive number of occasional or part-time **tax preparers** who may only moonlight during tax season or who might actually do much of the same kind of work as a full-time tax professional the year around.

Finally, there is an obscure and undetermined number of individuals with no certification, no organized professional association and, in some unfortunate instances, no particular expertise or sense of ethics. It is not difficult to imagine even the less imaginative bookies or gamblers, faced with that blank spot on IRS Form 1040, blithely penning in what would seem to be an innocuous title: accountant.

Whatever their professed title, the vast majority of those who call themselves accountants provide much-needed services to the country's business and financial communities and to hundreds of thousands of individuals. Imagine the countless small businesses whose proprietors and managers are too busy with running the day-to-day operations to bother with keeping even the most rudimentary set of books. By and large, these enterprises can't afford the services of high-priced CPA firms and, in many cases, it wouldn't be cost-effective to hire them if they could. Instead, they rely on bookkeepers, no less professional or necessary despite the lack of certification or title. Bookkeepers, after all, were the likely origin of the accounting profession, as we have seen, and they are certainly "accountants" in all but a certified sense today. Public accountants have a degree of certification. In some states they are licensed, while in others they are "grandfathered," the term used to describe those who had been licensed as a class of accountant that has been superseded by new classifications.

## Who Are the Certified Public Accountants?

For all practical purposes (and for the purpose of this book), it is **certified public accountants,** the top rung of the accounting profession, who comprise the most statistically detailed group of accountants. Actually, despite some educational and experience requirements, the only criteria that sets CPAs apart from other accountants is that they, one and all, have passed the Uniform CPA Examination and received from a state (or

**How Much Do Accountants Earn?**

As with any profession, salaries for public accoutants vary based on training, experience, region of the country and other factors. On the whole, annual salaries at all levels are considered competitive.

**Entry Level** accountants, those with less than a year of experience, earn approximately $24,000. **Staff accountants,** who have been working in the business for one to three years, earn roughly $28,000. **Senior accountants,** with from three to six years of experience, are paid an average of just over $34,000. **Managers,** who have six to nine years of experience, earn about $47,000. Salaries for partners frequently top six figures.

Not surprisingly, salaries in the Northeast and California tend be higher than the national average. The discrepancy is most profound at the profession's upper levels: Managers in New York, Boston, Los Angeles and San Francisco earn an average of $56,000, nearly 20 percent more than their professional brethren in the rest of the country.

Source: *Accounting Office Management & Adminstration Report*

states) the certification and license to practice. Just who are the CPAs? Fortunately, there is a fairly detailed breakdown of the membership of the American Institute of CPAs that gives us a pretty good idea.

In mid-1989, the AICPA membership totaled just over 282,000 individuals, or somewhere between two-thirds and three-quarters of all the CPAs in the country, by the institute's own estimation. CPAs in public practice—the individuals who practice with accounting firms, large and small—make up just under half of this total. Of this roughly 140,000 individuals, approximately 35,000 (25 percent) practice accounting as **sole**

**practitioners,** or one-person firms. Another 47,000 (34 percent) practice in firms that have from two to nine members; 23,000 (16 percent) practice in firms with ten or more members; and 35,000 (25 percent) are members of the twenty-five largest accounting firms.

But that's just the number of CPAs in public practice. More than half of the AICPA membership now consists of those not in public practice—that is, in industry, government or education. This is a statistic that has gradually changed over the last five years, 1986 being the year in which members in public practice became a minority of the institute's membership. A high number of CPAs in this non-practice category make up the memberships of the NAA, the AAA, the FEI and the IAA. These are the **treasurers** and **controllers,** the **internal accountants** and **management accountants** and the **internal auditors** and **systems managers** who, while possessing many of the same skills as CPAs in public practice, have chosen to use their talents in industry and business. A significant number of these individuals rise to the very top positions in their companies, as **chief financial officers** and even **chief executive officers**. More often, they are crucially important administrative and financial officers in medium- and large-size companies, even the giants of business and industry.

Almost 8,000 members of the AICPA work for municipal, state and federal government agencies. Some of these individuals rise to extremely high levels of government. The 101st Congress of the United States (1989-1990) numbered four CPAs among its members. At press time, the controller general of the United States, who heads the General Accounting Office, the investigative arm of Congress, was a CPA. The commissioner of the Internal Revenue Service during parts of the Carter and Reagan administrations was a CPA. Hundreds of CPAs work for federal agencies such as the Securities and Exchange Commission, the General Accounting Office and the Treasury Department and its subsidiary, the Internal Revenue Service. CPAs fill equally important positions at the state and local levels.

Finally, some 7,000 of the AICPA' s members are educators,

perhaps the most vital of all the roles filled by CPAs, as they are responsible for ensuring a continuing flow of entrants into the profession from the nation's undergraduate and postgraduate schools of business.

Although women made up only about 16 percent of the AICPA membership as of mid-1989, more than half of those students graduating from colleges and universities with accounting degrees in the late 1980s were women, a trend that shows no signs of reversing itself. Indeed, women have scored consistently high on the Uniform CPA Exam and have won with great regularity the Elijah Watts Sells Award for the highest score attained on that test. While very few women—less than 10 percent—have reached the level of partner in the large national and international accounting firms, they are nevertheless achieving highly responsible positions within their firms and state CPA societies as well as within the AICPA. It is only a matter of time until the highest ranks within public practice reflect the high percentage of women graduates from today's colleges and universities.

There are relatively few minority members in the profession, primarily, according to a prominent black CPA, because there are very few CPA role models for minority children. An annual survey of major accounting firms conducted by the AICPA shows approximately 350 black CPAs, and even fewer Hispanic, American Indian and Asian CPAs. The National Association of Black Accountants reports only 3,500, or about one percent of the total, black certified public accountants. Despite some significant scholarship assistance from the large accounting organizations and firms, the number of minority accounting graduates from colleges and universities does not begin to match the gains made by women.

Yet the statistical makeup and the demographic appearance of the profession is undergoing a metamorphosis. A casual observer at national accounting conferences, partners' meetings of the larger firms and other convocations of CPAs is certain to notice many more women, ethnic and international participants, and even an increasing representation of long

**What are accountants like?**

If the popular image of accountants is hardly heroic, what is the reality? What are accountants really like? Do they in fact maintain their professional demeanor no matter what the situation? Hardly. Accountants, if they are generally businesslike and conservative in appearance on the job, are just as likely to be anything but that on their own time, as is the case with most professions. Some cases in point:

In addition to congressmen, mayors and journalists, a Connecticut CPA races sports cars at Lime Rock and a Colorado accountant explores precipitous trails on a mountain bike. In Louisiana, a New Orleans CPA has launched a second career as a children's singer, appearing at schools, hospitals and even Storyland. A Kansas CPA, maybe the most daring of the lot, rides Brahma bulls in local rodeos. There are accountants who are, in their private lives, sailors, adventure travelers, sky divers, professional athletes and even one who runs a ghetto soup kitchen for the homeless. Groups of CPAs in a number of states have organized "1040" runs for charity, and one accountant yokes himself to seven other free spirits to run marathons together as a centipede—clocking in highly respectable times. Enterprising groups in Pennsylvania and Utah have formed CPA drill teams that march with briefcases and cadence calls in major parades, including New York's parade to honor the Statue of Liberty's one hundredth birthday.

hair and beards. Dark suits and white shirts are not ubiquitous; CPAs seem to have discovered color and even fashion in the last decade.

**The Best Regarded Profession in the Country?**

In 1986, as part of the public relations efforts leading up to the profession's centennial, the AICPA commissioned the well-known pollster Lou Harris and Associates to undertake a comprehensive survey of the perception of CPAs held by the public and by selected strata of the business and professional communities. The results gave the accountants high marks in ethics and morality, honesty, competence, reliability and objectivity. Indeed, Harris termed the profession "among the best regarded institutions in the country," one that was performing at an improving level of integrity despite an overall worsening of business morality.

However, CPAs did not measure up nearly as well in the area of "creativity." Harris observed that accountants might exhibit this apparent lack of creativity deliberately so as not to be thought of as "unreliable" or "unobjective." Certainly, CPAs would feel this way when wearing their auditing hats, for the last thing they wish to present to a skeptical public (or the SEC) is creativity in the area of attestation services.

If the demographic composition of the profession is changing, as seems evident, it is in no small way a reflection of the equally significant changes in the jobs that accountants, particularly CPAs, do. For the time-honored tasks that are traditionally thought of as the province of the profession are undergoing revolutionary changes as well.

# Chapter 3

# WHAT DO ACCOUNTANTS DO?

The headline in the *The New York Times* screamed: "Gun-Toting Accountants Battle Tax Cheats." The story that followed was a bit tamer, as it detailed the endeavors of a member of the criminal investigation division of the Internal Revenue Service (the organization that finally put Al Capone behind bars!). The point of the headline (and the story) was this: that accountants sometimes go about their business armed not with pencil, calculator and spread sheet but, in defiance of stereotype, with guns! Unusual? Not really; few professions possess a more stereotyped image than accountancy.

## Taxes

Play word-association games with ten people and a majority will answer "taxes" when the key word is "accountant." They're not wrong; accountants, lots of accountants, do nothing but tax work.

Ask someone who plays the stock market what an accountant does and the answer, most likely, will be "auditor." That answer is equally correct. Continue the game by asking people in increasingly specialized fields what they think it is that accountants do, and the answers will be increasingly disparate—and specialized—and they'll all be correct. In this day and age, accountants do so many different things that the stereotyped "accountant" literally defies definition, but first let's consider the stereotypes.

The most common one is that of the accountant as **tax preparer/professional/adviser**. Millions of individual and business tax returns are prepared every year (and several times a year for many businesses). According to the Internal Revenue Service, almost 50 million, or 46.9 percent of all 1988 individual returns, were prepared by someone other than the taxpayer, and that someone is most often an accountant.

Tax preparation, of course, is only a small part of a tax practice. For CPAs, in particular, considerable tax work goes on before and after tax season, that three-plus-month period from the first of the year until April 15. Because the tax code is so complex, and because it changes virtually every year, a huge amount of the tax practitioner's time is taken up with the studying of the laws and the accompanying regulations and interpretations issued by the IRS and the tax court. Some CPAs do nothing but study the rules so that they can teach their colleagues. In fact, many CPAs, concerned with the law's growing complexity, want to push through legislation that requires each member of Congress to do his or her own tax preparation. Only that way, the CPAs feel, will there be any hope of passing "simple" tax laws.

CPA tax practitioners (along with tax attorneys and other tax preparers known as enrolled agents) also represent their clients before the IRS and the tax courts. These are not particularly happy occasions, as they usually occur when the client has been called for an audit or is appealing an unfavorable IRS ruling. For more about accountants and taxes, see Chapter 9.

# Personal Financial Planning

Closely allied with the tax practitioner is the **personal financial planning specialist**. Quite often the two practices overlap. Personal financial planners, however, get into areas that tax people wouldn't dare become involved with: investment advice, insurance, retirement and estate planning and general money management. As in the case of taxes, CPAs provide these financial-planning services for individuals and businesses, although the emphasis seems to be on the former. For more about accountants and personal financial planning, see Chapter 10.

# Auditing

Accountants are also commonly known as **auditors,** although this particular function applies only to CPAs. The Securities and Exchange Commission demands an independent audit of all companies that offer their stock to the public (there are between 9,000 and 10,000 such companies), and CPA firms provide those audits every year. It is the auditor's opinion at the end of a company's financial statements, usually contained in the annual report, that guides the judgment of many investors.

Audits of most public companies, particularly the corporate giants of American business, are carried out by a small number of the largest accounting firms, popularly known as the "Big Eight." While the next-largest ten or fifteen firms also do a considerable amount of audit work, it is the Big Eight firms (see Chapter 4 for more about the Big Eight) that reap the largest fees and audit the largest companies. The work of the auditor is another area that has far-reaching implications and has engendered much attention from federal regulators. For more information on this, see Chapter 7.

# Management Advisory Services

An increasing part of a CPA firm's revenues in the late 1980s came from an area called management advisory services by the accounting profession, but simply management consulting, or consulting, by the outside world. Indeed, this new role as **management consultant** had such an impact on the profession that it was the direct cause of a radical restructuring of one of the largest of the Big Eight firms, Arthur Andersen and Company.

The situation at Andersen came to a head in early 1989. The company's consulting operations were bringing in more revenue than the audit and tax operations, but the consulting partners felt they were not being adequately compensated for these efforts. After a number of the top consulting partners left the firm to form their own independent consulting company, Andersen was reorganized to create what was, in effect, two separate companies, each with its own managing directors, partners and, presumably, compensation systems.

The more prosaic functions of the CPA management consultant involve establishing accounting and reporting systems for businesses, evaluating and predicting the results of operations, producing short- and long-range management plans and more. Increasingly, CPAs are helping select and install computer systems in large and small companies, and are even designing and providing the software to run these systems.

While these seem like logical extensions of certified public accountants' duties, given their assumed propensity for logical thinking, ability with numbers and general business knowledge, some of the roles being assumed by consultants seem somewhat more unusual, even bizarre. On the more conservative end of this scale we find CPAs conducting executive searches to put the right individuals into hard-to-fill slots in large companies. Other CPAs are climbing over oil wells and inspecting burned-out buildings in their quest for the knowledge that will help them advise clients in specific industries. Still others are providing part-time financial officers for private companies, or counseling a group of veterinarians; one even advised a pilots' union during the strike of a major national airline.

## Litigation Support

Yet another area in which the services of CPA specialists are becoming more prominent is called litigation support and is provided by large and small accounting firms alike. As its title suggests, the CPAs who are **litigation specialists** are literally supporting the litigation efforts of their clients by providing expert testimony in the courtroom as lawsuits are contested. Unknown just a few years ago, litigation support provides revenue for all the large firms, and some sole practitioners do nothing but this kind of work.

## Forensic Accounting

An entrepreneurial offshoot of litigation support is known as forensic accounting, for no logical reason other than that a CPA's services are usually recorded in a court of law. **Forensic accountants** usually testify in cases in which one party to the suit thinks the other is being less than honest about financial matters germane to the case. The forensic accountant investigates the suspected holdout's financial condition and is obligated to divulge any hidden finances, if uncovered, in sworn testimony. This type of service is most often applied in divorce cases, especially when one spouse owns his or her own business. The accountant must combine the skills of a detective with the tenacity of a bookkeeper to comb through a company's financial records and ferret out hidden funds.

These exotic sidelines of the profession are practiced by relatively few individuals in the overall scheme of the accounting world. On the other hand, all of the major areas of CPA activity—taxes, auditing and management consulting—can come into play when the CPA is serving small-business clients. In fact, services provided to small-business clients have almost become a specialty area for the larger firms. While this domain was generally left to the smaller accounting firms—the local and regional practice units that make up the majority of the firms in the country—that situation has changed dramatically. Virtually all the large national and international CPA firms have reacted to increased competition by setting up practice groups whose sole function is to bring in small-business clients.

All of the functions discussed so far are carried out by CPAs in public practice, working for themselves or for CPA firms. Not all CPAs are included in this group. In fact, a majority of the membership of the AICPA now comprises members in industry (working for employers in business and industry), government and education.

## CPAs in the Workplace

Those working for employers in the business and industrial workplace, for non-profit organizations and in many government agencies, do much of the same work as CPAs in public practice. These are the chief financial officers, the controllers and treasurers, internal auditors, chief accountants and their staffs and tax specialists—in short, the vital financial staff people without which business could not function. The larger the company, the more accountants on staff. While smaller companies can often afford to hire CPA firms to do some of this work, it simply is not cost-effective for large companies—thus, their often substantial internal accounting departments.

What specifically do these accountants do for their employers? Staff accountants, under the supervision of the controller and chief financial officer, prepare a company's financial statements, which in many cases will be subjected to the scrutiny of an independent auditor. Internal auditors monitor a company's efficiency, acting in the role of what used to be known as an "efficiency expert." Chief accountants set up and analyze accounting systems for inventories, expenses and accounts payable and receivable. Tax experts do what they have always done: attempt to fathom the current yearly edition of the tax laws and get their employers the best deals they can.

## CPAs in Government

CPAs also serve crucial roles in government, at the municipal, state and federal levels. Perhaps their most important function in government is to serve as the watchdog looking out for the well-being of citizens' tax dollars. But accountants play many different roles in the Treasury Department, the Securities and Exchange Commission, the General Accounting Office and the Federal Reserve, to name just a few of the more prominent federal agencies.

On the state and local levels, CPAs serve as **head of the department of revenue,** as **human resource administrators** and as **tax commissioners**. Inevitably, this proximity to elected officials prompts some CPAs to consider running for government office, and many are elected to high-level positions. There have been many members of state legislatures, mayors and other examples of successful accountant-politicians.

## CPAs in Education

One final, though no less vital, area in which CPAs are prominent is academia. There are approximately 7,000 CPAs currently teaching in the colleges, universities and business schools across the nation. In an age that sees different industries competing for the best and brightest products of the educational system, with many competing industries able to offer lucrative wages at the entry level, the role of the **accounting professor** becomes twofold. Not only must he or he teach the comprehensive facts that the student must master to graduate and subsequently pass the Uniform CPA Examination, but the academicians must also instill in the student the desire to enter a profession that might not seem to offer the attractions of others.

# Chapter 4

# HOW THE PROFESSION IS STRUCTURED

According to industry statistics, there are somewhere between 150,000 and 200,000 CPAs currently engaged in the practice of public accounting. They work for more than 40,000 independent public accounting firms with approximately 48,000 offices, or practice units, located in most towns and cities across the country. More than three-quarters of these firms consist of only one CPA, called a **sole practitioner**. While these are not the CPAs one immediately thinks of when the subject of accounting is raised, the average citizen in need of accounting help, of whatever kind, is more than likely to seek out one of these sole practitioners, or else a CPA in one of the 5,000 or so small firms of less than ten professionals.

The reasons are several and simple:

• The sole and small-firm practitioners are located primarily, but not exclusively, in the smaller towns and cities (although they also practice in urban as well as rural areas).

• They know the local business conditions and the local businesses.

• They provide quick, efficient and, above all, personal service at rates that are generally somewhat below those charged by the larger regional and national firms.

This class of accountant has long labored at a distinct disadvantage, based as much on local myth as any kind of conscious social discrimination. The myth is that the sole practitioners and small firms aren't as capable as the big firms. This misperception is given substance, for example, by local banks that will suggest to potential creditors that they have their balance sheets examined by a large firm. Or, in some unfortunate cases, the myth is perpetuated by large-firm advertising that pointedly offers the varied expertise of its "large professional staffs."

The truth is that the expertise of all these individual CPAs is quite similar; after all, they all passed the same examination to become CPAs. Very often, moreover, sole practitioners or those practicing in small firms have worked previously for large firms but have left, perhaps because they wanted the opportunity to be on their own, to work more closely with their clients on a personal basis or, in all truth, because they saw the road to a partnership in the large firm as too long and arduous a journey. (More about this career path appears in Chapter 5.)

Many of the small firms are solely tax practices. They are busiest, of course, between January 1 and April 15, but they have plenty to do during the remainder of the year—filing quarterly tax reports and payroll taxes for local businesses and, increasingly, doing tax consulting and maybe some personal financial planning for individuals.

Other firms provide basic accounting services, including bookkeeping, often becoming specialists in local or regional industries such as farming, logging, restaurants or manufacturing.

Some small firms are as versatile as the Big Eight. They will do tax preparation in the busy season, a bit of consulting and a variety of **attest work**. This last, called attest work because the auditor is attesting to the veracity of the financial statements, is also called "write-up" work because the accountants are actually writing up an opinion of the statements. (Attest work consists of audits, compilations and reviews, which will be discussed in more detail in Chapter 6.) These practitioners are the free spirits of the profession and could never be happy working in a big firm.

## The Big Eight

At the other end of the spectrum are the well-known **Big Eight.** These huge international firms can consist of as many as 2,000 partners, the elite positions toward which all practitioners strive yet many fail to achieve. According to industry statistics, they employ more than 100,000 individuals in the United States alone, and enjoy a combined domestic revenue in the area of $8 billion. Their combined international revenue approaches a staggering $20 billion.

The Big Eight are:

- Arthur Andersen & Company
- Coopers & Lybrand
- Deloitte Haskins & Sells
- Ernst & Whinney
- KMG Peat Marwick Main
- Price Waterhouse
- Touche Ross
- Arthur Young & Company

In the 1980s there were a number of mergers between Big Eight firms, and between Big Eight firms and so-called "second tier" firms, the next largest in size. In 1985, Peat Marwick Mitchell merged with the second-tier firm KMG Main Hurdman to become the largest accounting firm in the United States, surpassing Arthur Andersen.

# THE BIG EIGHT

**Ranked by U.S. revenues (in millions of dollars)**

| | 1988 | 1987 | % | | | Revenue / Professional | | 1988 | 1987 | % |
|---|---|---|---|---|---|---|---|---|---|---|
| | U.S. Revenue | | Growth | Offices | Partners | Partner# | Staff | International Revenue | | Growth |
| Arthur Andersen | $1,710 | $1,513 | 13.0% | 82 | 1,227 | $1,394 | 18,519 | $2,820 | $2,316 | 21.8% |
| Peat Marwick Main | 1,639 | 1,458 | 12.4 | 102 | 1,933 | 848 | 14,879 | 3,900 | 3,250 | 20.0 |
| Ernst & Whinney | 1,174 | 1,036 | 13.3 | 110 | 1,280 | 917 | 11,530 | 2,191 | 1,778 | 23.2 |
| Coopers & Lybrand | 1,141 | 982 | 16.2 | 100 | 1,270 | 898 | 10,778 | 2,495 | 2,074 | 20.3 |
| Price Waterhouse | 960 | 848 | 13.2 | 114 | 870 | 1,103 | 10,000 | 2,200 | 1,750 | 25.7 |
| Arthur Young | 843 | 738 | 14.2 | 92 | 889 | 948 | 7,700 | 2,053 | 1,702 | 20.6 |
| Deloitte Haskins & Sells | 820 | 701 | 17.0 | 111 | 853 | 961 | 8,000 | 1,920 | 1,536 | 25.0 |
| Touche Ross | 796 | 683 | 16.5 | 85 | 774 | 1,028 | 7,254 | 1,840 | 1,450 | 26.9 |

Source: *Bowman's Accounting Report* (figures for 1988)

**The Accounting Profession's "Second Tier"**

| | U.S. Revenue (millions) | Offices | Partners |
|---|---|---|---|
| Laventhol & Horwath | $306 | 54 | 460 |
| Grant Thornton | $200 | 54 | 341 |
| BDO Seidman | $157 | 49 | 316 |
| McGladrey & Pullen | $139 | 70 | 380 |
| Kenneth Leventhal & Company | $126 | 12 | 61 |
| Pannell Kerr Forster | $ 87 | 33 | 125 |
| Spicer & Oppenheim | $ 70 | 9 | 97 |

Source: *Bowman's Accounting Report* (figures for 1988)

The national firms are also expanding their bases in new areas by taking over regional and even local firms to build up their small business clientele. The reason, of course, is that competition is getting tougher and the giants can no longer afford to ignore markets that they once left to the local firms. They are also turning more and more frequently to marketing tactics such as advertising and public relations, activities that were virtually taboo as little as ten years ago. For instance, some firms have taken to sponsoring television shows, especially sporting events such as the Olympic games. Likewise, one big firm sponsors a regular classical music radio show in New York City. Meanwhile, the second-tier firms are getting much more aggressive with their advertising, running campaigns in national newspapers and consumer magazines.

To become a partner in a Big Eight firm is to have reached what many consider the pinnacle of the accounting profession, complete with status in one's firm and the profession and a six-figure income. Not that many make it, and those who do will normally have taken seven to nine years to do so, often relocating from city to city to broaden their experience or lend their expertise where needed. For a look at the typical Big Eight career path, see the box on pages 34-35.

So far, not many of those who have made it to the position of partner are women or minorities. The best representation is from Arthur Andersen—twenty-eight female partners out of a total of 1,227 partners as of mid-1989. This is becoming an ever more contentious issue, underscored as recently as May 1989 by a Supreme Court decision brought by a woman who had been passed over for partner at Price Waterhouse. The high court ruled that the burden of proof lay with the firm, that it had to prove it had not discriminated against the plaintiff because she was a woman. There is little doubt that the larger firms are serious about correcting the imbalance of the sexes. Still, while women are entering the profession in ever greater amounts, it will be a number of years yet before they approach parity in terms of numbers of partners.

The Big Eight, the "second tier" and, indeed, all the national and large regional firms play a vital role in the country's financial community. It is the CPAs from these firms who audit virtually all of the publicly traded companies in the United States, who prepare the corporate tax returns of a high percentage of the business concerns, who are on the leading edge of consulting technology. Not only are these professionals the conscience of the business world, they are key advisers to the staff aides and congressional representatives who write the laws under which the country's business and commercial concerns operate. Their knowledge and expertise is vast. Their dedication is boundless. Their ethics, by and large, are impeccable.

At the same time, the local firms see a bright future and continue to hold on to their traditional clients, small business, while attracting enough recruits to get the job done. As is the case with the big firms, they, too, are broadening their areas of expertise and becoming involved in different kinds of work with different types of clients. The individuals who staff the local and regional firms, as well as the thousands of sole practitioners, are easily the equal of their colleagues in the large firms in expertise and ethics.

# Chapter 5

# HOW TO BECOME AN ACCOUNTANT

According to the AICPA, about 140,000 would-be accountants sat for the Uniform CPA Examination in 1989, quite possibly the highest number ever. Most of these candidates will probably become CPAs—eventually—because few of them will pass the four parts of the exam on the first attempt. Certainly, all these aspiring accountants are not alike in anything more than their desire to pass the exam and get on with the business of making a living. They don't have the same ambitions, they don't have the same career plans and obviously they don't have the same talents or capabilities.

Tradition has it that the accountant is a numbers freak—dull, unimaginative and content to pore over endless columns of figures for hours at a time. Those who go on to become accountants were very likely the mathematical geniuses as students in elementary and high school.

The very opposite is more the case. All the current literature for students who wish to enter the profession—the AICPA curriculum guide, Big Eight career guides and more general occupational handbooks—stresses the fact that those who strive for well-rounded, comprehensive educations, strongly accenting the liberal arts and sciences, are most likely to succeed as practicing accountants. That's because the industry consensus about the qualities recognized as desirable in a CPA are as follows:

- gregariousness
- an analytical mind
- a fondness for problem-solving
- an ability to communicate well with others

What does this mean, then, for that lucky individual who knows he or she wants to be a CPA? Most educators agree that the normal college preparatory program—two or three years of high school math and, ideally, communications and writing courses—is appropriate. Once the student enters college, the various accounting organizations have done some systematic studies that pretty much lay out the educational requirements for entry into the profession. It is important to note that the changes in how CPAs work and in what they do are generating the need for equally comprehensive changes in education.

That the profession itself is changing is no surprise. The growing complexity of the economy and the businesses that generate it is one cause. Accountants now work in a global environment rather than within the constraints of a city, state or country. International accounting standards, trade laws and the prevailing political realities all add to the mix.

Another factor is the increasing reliance on technology, especially the use of computers, that is forcefully asserting itself on the profession. Computer-generated data is now used by clients to supply accountants with do much of the information they incorporate into audits—leaving no "paper trail." Accounting firms themselves use new, sophisticated software programs to do much of the number crunching once done by hand. This, in turn, has freed up many employees to do other client-related work. Looking way into the future, the industry has expressed some interest in the artificial intelligence that computer technology could make possible.

Fortunately, those whose efforts are focused entirely on the overall profession have seen the need for a reevaluation and redirection of accounting education at the college level.

## Accounting Education—the 150-Hour Program

In 1988, the AICPA issued its "Plan to Restructure Professional Standards," an initiative aimed at upgrading membership requirements, improving the overall quality of practice by members and enhancing the image of the profession in the eyes of the general public. An unstated motive was to relieve the pressure being applied to accounting firms and the institute by several powerful and influential members of Congress. The main thrust of the plan was that 150 hours of undergraduate education, including a baccalaureate degree, be required for membership in the AICPA, beginning in the year 2000. What this means in practice is that students hoping to become accountants now need, in all likelihood, *five* years of college education (or the equivalent credits), instead of the customary four. The rationale behind the measure was that the usual 120-hour college curriculum—30 hours per year—simply wasn't sufficient time to encompass the body of knowledge a student must possess to be able to work effectively as a CPA.

With the initiation of the 150-hour requirement, there was an immediate need to reevaluate the AICPA's opinion of the necessary educational requirements for entry into the profession. In late 1988, the institute published an updated version of *Education Requirements for Entry into the Accounting Profession*, which contained the most comprehensive effort to address this question to date. As the report states: "A strong general education for accountants is important because the services of CPAs have expanded beyond the traditional focus on financial statements."

According to the program, students should devote sixty to eighty semester hours—the equivalent of at least the combined freshman and sophomore years of college—to the study of elementary accounting, economics, mathematics and statistics, computers, behavioral sciences, communications and ethics. It suggests that electives taken during this period include history, philosophy, literature, arts, humanities and sciences.

If ethics sounds like a surprising part of the program, that, too, is an indication of how things have changed. As the report states: "Fundamental to a profession is the obligation of its members to maintain the highest standards of ethical conduct. A sense of responsibility to society . . . should be acquired very early in the educational process and can begin with the nurturing of moral and ethical values."

The concentration on communication is perhaps not so unexpected, given a CPA's constant need to disseminate information and communicate clearly with clients, government agents and colleagues.

Business administration, the second educational segment of the AICPA's recommended program, would seem to bring the student to a crucial point. It is during this period of thirty-five to fifty semester hours—the junior year and part of the senior year—that the student must decide whether to pursue seriously the accounting curriculum or to consider another career track. This period of study should include:

- economics (theory and monetary system)
- legal and social environment of business
- business law
- marketing
- finance
- organization
- group and individual behavior
- quantitative applications in business
- business ethics
- communications

The final twenty-five to forty semester hours—the remainder of the senior year plus the fifth year—see the student focusing on specific areas of accounting, courses that directly prepare the fledgling candidate for the Uniform CPA Examination.

During this period, the emphasis is on:

- financial accounting theory and applied financial accounting problems
- management accounting, to include accounting for decision making, cost determination and analysis and management accounting controls
- tax theory and tax problems
- audit theory and practice, including the computer in auditing, audit problems and case studies

Also recommended is the study of information systems and professional ethics and responsibilities. If time permits, the student is encouraged to participate in internships and cooperative programs.

## The Hierarchy in a Large Accounting Firm Is Quite Well Structured

At the lowest level, **staff accountant**, a newcomer to a firm will work under close supervision. College graduates fill most of these positions, and do the basic paperwork in areas such as tax, accounting or auditing. After two or three years on the job, staff accountants will have probably decided what area of the firm's work they want to "specialize" in and will also start to have responsibility for the supervision of newer staff accountants.

The next step up is **senior accountant**, called a **supervisor** in some firms. As the title suggests, people in these positions exercise more supervisory authority over a number of staff accounts.

This position is followed by **manager**. A manager normally has overall responsibility for several jobs at one time and also interfaces directly with clients.

The position of **senior manager** comes next and is the last step, or hurdle, before an individual becomes a **partner**. Senior managers exercise considerable respon-

The AICPA report had been out for less than a year when the American Accounting Association, whose members consist of accounting faculty and academicians, initiated a program to develop major changes in accounting education. The AAA received a five-year grant of $4 million from the Big Eight accounting firms to carry out this study and put a new accounting curriculum in place at institutions accredited by the American Assembly of Collegiate Schools of Business. Authorship of this short treatise, *Perspectives on Education: Capabilities for Success in the Accounting Profession*, was credited to the chief executives of the Big Eight firms—among the acknowledged leaders of the profession, figures whose opinion carries considerable weight. They, too, cite the same basic reason for reexamining the accounting curriculum: the complexities of business and corresponding expansion of the

---

sibility and meet frequently with clients. They are also expected to contribute to the effort to attract new business to the firm.

Becoming a **partner** is the level all CPAs in public practice aim for. In addition to acquiring ownership status in the firm (which is almost always in the form of a partnership), partners will have responsibility for interpreting technical standards and guidelines, applying these standards to specific cases and, more and more often, seeking to attract new business. As one's seniority as a partner increases, he or she may be put in charge of all of a firm's business in one area or may take on specialized assignments as the need arises.

(Additionally, some firms have a level called "principal," which is partner level for those individuals who are not CPAs.)

The top job is held by a **managing partner;** the larger firms generally have a managing partner for each practice unit, or office. This top person is sometimes called **chairman** or **chief executive**.

---

CPA's responsibilities as well as the AICPA 150-hour requirement. But they add another reason: a perceived declining enrollment in accounting programs, which they see as an indication that the accounting profession "is becoming less attractive to students."

The 1988 survey, *Supply of Accounting Graduates and Demand for Their Services by Public Accounting Firms*, published annually by the AICPA, agrees that fewer accounting majors are graduating. However, the larger totals of those sitting for the Uniform CPA Examination might also suggest that more students with non-accounting degrees are entering the profession. In all likelihood, this statistical paradox won't be resolved for another few years. But the obvious message is that the accounting curriculum will undergo extensive scrutiny in the short-term future.

It's important to note that if you're a reader who completed college with 120 credit hours, you'll need to get the additional schooling. Likewise, if your major was music but you're about to switch careers and get into accounting, your college credits are still good toward the 150-hour requirement even if you don't have the recommended assortment of accounting-related course work. What it boils down to is this: To become a CPA, one must pass the Uniform CPA Exam. How one goes about obtaining the required expertise is up to the individual.

## The Uniform CPA Examination

This two-day, four-part marathon is one of the most arduous professional examinations given anywhere in the world. A very small percentage of candidates who take the exam for the first time pass all four parts at one sitting. The reason is probably not that the questions are so hard. Rather, as those who are concerned with the curriculum point out, the overall body of knowledge being tested is so comprehensive that pulling all that information out of a fatigued mind is simply an overly daunting task. Those candidates who are determined to pass the test almost always succeed, since most boards of accountancy (which administer the examination) permit candidates to take the parts they have previously failed over again if they have passed at least two parts on the first attempt (this rule differs slightly from state to state).

Just what is this formidable test of would-be CPAs? It's given twice a year, in May and November, in all fifty-four jurisdictions (the fifty states, the District of Columbia, Puerto Rico, the U.S. Virgin Islands and Guam). Until 1990, it took two and a half days to complete the five sections, which included two parts of accounting theory, auditing, business law and accounting theory. The test consisted of 60 percent multiple-choice questions and 40 percent essay-type questions, with the essay questions asking the candidate to elaborate on particular situations. Each year, the AICPA, which prepares and grades the examination, publishes an outline of questions and answers from previous exams to help the next crop of students prepare.

In mid-1989, the board of examiners of the AICPA was preparing to implement changes in the format of the exam, reducing the length from two and a half days to two, and increasing the percentage of multiple-choice questions. In a daring breakthrough, candidates would also be permitted to use hand-held calculators, previously forbidden.

The primary purpose of the examination is not just to test candidates' technical abilities in the four areas, but to assure, insofar as it is possible, that those individuals who eventually are awarded CPA certificates will perform for the greater good—that is, in the public interest. This can only be achieved—at least to a good measure, assumes the AICPA—if the candidates are technically competent in, at the very least, these four basic areas.

(For those interested in the specific content outline of the Uniform CPA Examination, the AICPA offers a booklet, *Information for CPA Candidates*, as well as the publication containing questions and answers from previous exams. Write to AICPA, Relations with Education Division, 1211 Avenue of the Americas, New York, NY 10036.)

The passing grade on each of the four sections is seventy-five, although some exams are marked on a curve, depending on the overall performance of all those taking the test. While multiple-choice questions are graded by optical scanner, the essay questions are graded by CPAs who volunteer their services to the AICPA specifically for that purpose. Individual tests sometimes receive four separate levels of grading in order to ensure a thorough review (and sometimes to give the benefit of the doubt) to borderline papers.

Not surprisingly, there is a veritable industry of educators at various levels who offer their services to help prospective exam-takers prepare. Many of these are of the mail-order variety. Much of the necessary material, of course, will have been mastered by accounting majors. Nevertheless, an example of what the AICPA recommends in the way of source material is dauntingly impressive:

• pronouncements of the Financial Accounting Standards Board

• statements on auditing standards

• the AICPA Code of Conduct

• statements on accounting and review services, quality control standards, management advisory services and responsibilities in tax practice

• AICPA audit and accounting guides

• the Internal Revenue Service Code and income-tax regulations

• pronouncements of the Governmental Accounting Standards Board

• statements of the National Council on Governmental Accounting and of the Municipal Finance Officers Association of the United States and Canada

• federal statutes such as the Securities Acts of 1933 and 1934, Bankruptcy Code, Uniform Commercial Code, Uniform Partnership Act, Uniform Limited Partnership Act and Model Business Corporation Act

The number of accounting majors graduating from college peaked at almost 60,000 from the years 1983 to 1984, and it has been tapering off since then, according to the AICPA's annual survey. At the same time, the demand for the services of these graduates by public accounting firms has increased, and while the firms can't hire all of these graduates, forcing some to seek jobs in business and government, the job outlook for graduates is rosy. It's important to note that one does not have to pass the exam in order to get an accounting job. Indeed, many people go years—and sometimes forever—without passing, while still working as accountants (though, of course, they are not certified public accountants).

To fill these positions, all the major accounting firms and many of the smaller regional firms recruit actively on local campuses, beginning in the fall of the senior year. The Big Eight firms, as might be expected, are the most competitive, offer the highest starting salaries and are often the first choice of many students who, arguably, believe the opportunities for training are better at these firms. The smaller companies are particularly active in the spring of the senior year, when the competition has slackened off, but they also are a presence on campus in the fall.

There are also a number of executive recruiting firms which specialize in finding qualified people who are looking for jobs and placing those candidates in accounting firms where certain positions need to be filled. The most notable of these is Robert Half and Associates, which is located in most big cities in the country. These accounting-profession "headhunters" confine most of their activities to middle and higher level executive positions. For jobs at the entry level, look to the firms themselves; most large- and medium-sized companies handle their own recruiting.

Lest this body of information—or the exam itself—be seen as overly intimidating, keep in mind the fact that the profession increases in number between 12,000 and 20,000 individuals annually, based on the average annual increase in AICPA membership. As challenging as the exam may be, those who are qualified pass with little difficulty.

## CPE, or, It Isn't Over When It's Over

Although the obstacle of the Uniform CPA Examination has been overcome, experience and other requirements have been met and the certificate and license to practice has been granted, this doesn't mean that a CPA is finished studying. In order to maintain that license, virtually all jurisdictions require the annual completion of varying amounts of continuing professional education (CPE). The standard amount is forty hours. Originally intended only for those CPAs in public practice, the AICPA modified its membership requirements in 1988 to include industry members as well.

Various bodies provide CPE courses, and there exists a dizzying variety of means by which to satisfy the annual requirement. There are home-study courses, videos, seminars and conferences in any number of subjects and specialities. The AICPA, state CPA societies and independent organizations all market CPE products competitively, and individuals are not terribly hard-pressed to find courses in their areas of interest. The philosophy behind continuing professional education in the accounting profession seems very definitely to be that one is never too old to learn. Given the endless change and the continuing expansion of areas in which the profession works, this philosophy would seem to be accurate and appropriate.

# Chapter 6

# WHAT IS AN AUDIT, ANYWAY?

What is an audit? Quite simply, an audit is an examination of a company's financial statements to see whether they fairly present the company's financial position, the results of its operations and cash flows, in conformance with generally accepted accounting principles. After performing the audit, the auditor offers an opinion as to whether the financial statements are presented fairly. This opinion (and the financial statements themselves) is normally included at the end of a company's annual report, which is made available to potential investors and, of course, is sent to all shareholders. In that context, an auditor's opinion becomes a valuable investment tool. (When we speak of audits here, we mean examinations of the financial statements of publicly traded companies. For a discussion of personal tax audits, see Chapter 9.)

Audits are required by the Securities and Exchange Commission of all publicly traded companies (these audits can be performed only by certified public accountants), and are also commonly used by banks and other credit grantors when deciding whether to make loans. Audits are sometimes required of banks and other financial institutions, depending on the regulations under which the institution operates, and are almost always required of any state or local government agency that receives federal funding.

Of all the sometimes arcane things accountants do, by far the least understood is the audit. In fact, misconceptions about what an audit is supposed to be are so widespread as to be almost universal outside the accounting profession and for those who don't make real use of them.

This would seem to be so for several reasons, the first of which is that relatively few people ever need to use an audit. A second reason is that many of those who might rely on an auditor's opinion to make an investment decision don't bother to read the financial statements so as to have something to relate that opinion to. Finally, certain vociferous critics of the accounting profession, while they may actually know what an audit entails, really want it to be something else.

## What an Audit *Isn't*

The easiest way to explain an audit is to enumerate some of the things an audit *is not*:

- First and foremost, an audit is not a certification of the financial statements or a seal of approval that the company is financially sound.

- Second, while the audit is the work of the independent auditor, the financial statements themselves are the product and the responsibility of the company's management.

- Third, an audit is not an indication that the company's financial statements are necessarily accurate to the exact dollar.

- Finally, and most emphatically, an "unqualified" or "clean opinion" by the auditor is neither an endorsement of the company as an investment nor a guarantee that the company might not soon suffer financial reversals or even fail.

## Who's Responsible for What?

As we have seen, the preparation of the financial statements is the responsibility of a company's management, although auditors sometimes help prepare them. The figures that go into those statements, however, are usually produced and prepared by the internal accounting staff, in a large company, or by bookkeepers or an administrative staff in a smaller one. While the independent auditor tests these figures—the transactions, inventories and other commercial acts that produce the figures—he or she does so on a selected basis. It would be prohibitively expensive, both in dollars and time (which are synonomous for accounting firms), for the auditor to test all such transactions.

What are the auditor's responsibilities? It all depends on who's describing those responsibilities.The former Chief Justice of the United States Supreme Court, Warren Burger, wanted auditors to be "public watchdogs" and to blow the whistle whenever an error or illegal act was uncovered. Congressman John Dingell (Democrat, Michigan) wishes that the auditor not only uncover fraud, but also provide total assurance that the financial statements accurately present a company's health.

The accounting profession's response is that these are unreasonable demands. If auditors were to be "public watchdogs," the auditor-client relationship would become an adversarial one resulting in a less-than-candid relationship which neither the auditor nor the client can afford. While admitting that their duties had always included uncovering fraud, the profession nevertheless answered Congressman Dingell that they could only provide reasonable assurance about the financial statements. In no way could they do so about a company's financial health because it was influenced by economic and market conditions that the auditor could not measure. Auditors also proclaimed that they were not trained as detectives and so could not readily ferret out acts of fraud when management was colluding with others who had a business relationship with the company.

The profession especially attacked the contention that the failure of a business that had undergone an audit, perhaps even soon after it had received a clean opinion from an auditor, necessarily meant that an audit failure had occurred. In testimony before the Oversight and Investigations Subcommittee of the House Energy and Commerce Committee (at press time Congressman Dingell was chairman of both bodies) in March 1985, AICPA President Philip B. Chenok stated, "Businesses fail for a variety of reasons that are unrelated to the financial reporting process. Poor management, social or technological developments, domestic and foreign competition, and changes in the economy are some of the major causes of business failures."

Still, a series of spectacular business failures from 1985 through 1988 threw gasoline on the congressional fires, prompted Congressman Dingell to carry on hearings into the accounting profession (see Chapter 7) and provided copious grist for the mills of financial and business writers who, almost invariably, led off their stories with screaming headlines such as "Where Were the Auditors?" As recently as April 1989, that very headline topped the front page of the Sunday Business section of *The New York Times* as yet another writer zeroed in, this time in relation to massive failures of savings-and-loan institutions in the Southwest. Penn Square, Drysdale, ESM Government Securities, Continental Bank and, more recently, ZZZ Best are names with which the readers of business pages are familiar. So are accountants, for they were blamed for some of the responsibility in all of them (justifiably so in the case of ESM Government Securities; that auditor is now in prison). Since an accounting firm is usually the only solvent party in the wake of a business failure, the firms that conducted the audits of these business concerns were very often sued by investors and creditors trying to recoup lost finances.

The major accounting firms cited in these cases almost

always decided, perhaps following the advice of legal counsel or insurance companies, to settle out of court. (The one notable exception was Ernst & Whinney, which contested a lawsuit in the Continental Illinois case that came to trial in 1988. The accounting firm was absolved of all blame in that failure.) AICPA President Chenok pointed out that "payments made by CPA firms in settlement of lawsuits are not proof of an audit failure. Such payments may be made simply because they are less than the potential legal and other costs of defending . . . " As a result of these suits, insurance premiums for liability insurance for all accounting firms went up precipitously during 1986 and 1987.

## Auditing Standards

The congressional hearings and the lawsuits served to emphasize that the meaning of the audit and the role of the auditor were still very much misunderstood by a variety of parties. The accounting profession finally took the offensive in attempting not only to clear up the confusion, but also to bolster the impact and quality of the audit itself. They did so by carrying out a comprehensive overhaul of auditing standards, the guidelines used by the auditor in actually conducting the audit.

As noted earlier, the Securities Acts of 1933 and 1934 provided the basis for what came to be known as independent audits carried out by certified public accountants. During the years immediately following passage of those acts, there were no uniform guidelines the auditors could follow. This changed in 1937 with the first major business failure to involve accountants, the McKesson & Robbins case. Although the auditors in that case, Price Waterhouse, and the accounting profession emerged relatively unscathed from hearings conducted by the SEC, those hearings did demand that a set of standards or principles be put into place, a demand with which the American Institute of Accountants was already in the process of complying. The result was a body of guidelines that came to be known as Generally Accepted Auditing Standards, or, as the profession is acronymically wont to do, GAAS.

However, GAAS provided the auditor only with direction on how to carry out the audit of the financial statements. There was still no set of guiding principles in the preparation of the financial statements. In fact, work in this area had commenced as early as 1934 and had proceeded haphazardly under the direction of an AIA body called the committee on accounting procedure. It was not until 1957 that recognition of the need for a research-type body to devote itself solely to the examination and dissemination of a body of Generally Accepted Accounting Principles, or GAAP, mustered enough support to result, two years later, in the inception of the **Accounting Principles Board (APB)**. The opinions of the APB gradually gained more authority until, in 1964, any deviation from GAAP had to be disclosed and justified.

However, a little over ten years ago, the profession first came under the examination of a congressional committee, which caused a crisis of sorts in the relationship between CPAs and the federal government (which will be examined more closely in Chapter 7) and which led to the demise of the Accounting Principles Board. Partly to persuade Congress that accountants are best regulated from within their field, but realizing that the Accounting Principles Board was too close to the profession as an arm of the AICPA, it was decided to create an independent rule-making body to take over the generation and review of generally accepted accounting principles. Thus was born the **Financial Accounting Standards Board**, or **FASB**. From its present headquarters in Norwalk, Connecticut, FASB has continued to formulate and revise GAAP in much the same way as did the APB. FASB has been successful in preserving its independence and has also put into place a mechanism through which it gets input from the business community.

Generally accepted auditing standards, in actuality, are no more than three sets of three or four very general guidelines as to who should be conducting audits and how they should be done. In all, there are ten very simple rules. GAAS covers, for example:

• **general standards:** the person doing the audit should be qualified and independent and should take care in doing the work

• **standards of fieldwork:** the work should be adequately planned and supervised, and the auditor should understand the company's internal control system and test a sufficient number of the company's operations and transactions

• **standards of reporting:** whether the financial statements are prepared in accordance with GAAP and identify elements that are not so prepared, that enough information is disclosed in the financial statements and, finally, the crucial auditor's opinion

It should be noted that there are two lesser degrees of examination that the auditor can perform, **compilations** and **reviews**. The difference in the three services primarily involves the degree of assurance the auditor provides as to whether the financial statements conform with GAAP.

An audit, of course, provides the highest degree of assurance, termed by the auditor "reasonable assurance" that the company's financial statements are free from fraud and misstatement.

Reviews provide a lesser degree of assurance, since the auditor does not perform tests of details or of internal controls but only makes inquiries of the company's personnel and performs "analytical procedures" so as to be able to provide "limited assurance" that no significant changes would have to be made to the financial statements to conform to GAAP.

Compilation, on the other hand, provides no assurance whatsoever. All the auditor does during a compilation is take figures provided by management and put them in the general physical form of financial statements. There is no assurance that these figures conform with GAAP.

As we have seen, full-scale audits are required by the Securities and Exchange Commission for all publicly traded companies—that is, all companies whose securities are traded on the various stock exchanges. Compilation and reviews are used when a party does not need as high a degree of assurance about a company's finances. Banks may be satisfied with reviews, or even compilations, when they are deciding whether to grant a loan to a company. A supplier might look at a compilation in granting credit terms. In all probability, many investors also rely on compilations and reviews.

While these other attest services have their uses, those who make it their business to monitor annual reports, stockholder reports and financial statements rely almost exclusively on the report and opinion of the independent auditor, the CPA. Because of this, the standard opinion that comes at the end of every audit takes on a significance of its own, above and beyond that of the financial statements themselves. In fact, many people who term themselves sophisticated about financial statements don't ever read them; all they read is the auditor's opinion at the end.

In fact, until 1989, they didn't really even have to read the opinion; all they had to do was count the number of paragraphs in that opinion. If there were more than two paragraphs, there was something the matter and the auditor's report was "qualified." (Sometimes the accounting profession can get into semantic trouble. The auditor's report is a good example. Most people think of the term "unqualified" as having negative connotations. Not the auditor. An unqualified opinion is the same as a "clean" opinion. "Qualified," on the contrary, means that the auditor has qualified the opinion—there is something wrong.)

Prior to 1989, the auditor could qualify the opinion if the financial statements were in conformity with GAAP "except for" a particular situation, or if the figures in the financial statements were "subject to" some future development that the auditor, of course, could not predict. These two situations called for the inclusion of a third paragraph explaining the qualification. The auditor can also qualify the opinion when it is impossible to amass the necessary evidence to conduct the audit. An additional paragraph, called a "scope limitation," would be added to the opinion in this case. Of course, the opinion could state that the financial statements were not prepared in conformity with GAAP, called an "adverse" opinion, or the auditor could even say that it was impossible to form an opinion, termed a "disclaimer." In actual practice, one rarely sees an adverse opinion because the situation is so drastic that, upon being informed by the auditor that such an opinion is imminent, the company would always take the necessary corrective action.

Nowhere in the opinion did, or does, the auditor ever even hint that the company is healthy financially, is well run or would be a good investment. In short, the auditor's report is not a "seal of approval." That was the case leading up to 1989, when the profession substantially revised the application of GAAS and significantly changed the format of the auditor's report. It remains the case even after the inception of, what were for auditors if not for readers of financial statements, momentous events.

We have read briefly about Congressman Dingell and the activities of his House Subcommittee on Oversight and Investigations (and we shall read more in Chapter 7.) These congressional hearings, which commenced in 1985 and lasted for three years, quickened the pace at which the FASB completed and acted on the most substantial revision of GAAS since their inception. In fairness to the profession, the FASB had begun its reexamination of auditing standards before Congressman Dingell swung into action. But the board was proceeding at what is a normal pace for the profession, best characterized as deliberate, owing primarily to a due-process routine that allows for review, comment, discussion and reexamination several times and at several levels in the accounting hierarchy.

Nevertheless, an unprecedented overhaul was in progress. The Financial Accounting Standards Board had determined that a revamping of auditing standards was necessary in several areas:

- the manner in which companies conducted business
- the financial instruments they were likely to use in the process of conducting business
- the relative ease by which unscrupulous managements could get away with fraud
- the continuing naiveté on the part of financial-statement

users who persisted in the unfounded belief that an unqualified auditor's report was a guarantee against a company's failing

The means by which the profession changes GAAS is through issuing more detailed guidance as to how the basic standards are to be applied, and they do this with documents called **Statements on Auditing Standards (SAS)**. In late 1988, the Auditing Standards Board approved for issue nine new SASs that constituted the most thorough revision of GAAS since they were formulated.

In some areas, the new SASs were extremely technical. In others, however, they were fairly basic. Probably the most basic was in spelling out the auditor's responsibility for finding fraud, the key to the screaming headlines and the congressional investigations. After pointedly disclaiming any responsibility for the preparation of the financial statements—they are solely the responsibility of a company's management—SAS acknowledges that the auditor does have a responsibility to plan and carry out the audit "with an attitude of professional skepticism" and the goal of providing "reason able assurance" that the financial statements are free of fraud. The new statement mandates an explicit duty to search for fraud by reducing the risk that the financial statements are materially incorrect. The old statement had outlined an implicit duty that could be interpreted thusly: If the auditor stumbled across fraud, he had to do something about it.

The other new auditing standards pertain to:

- how the auditor should consider the possibility that the client is committing illegal acts

- consideration of the company's internal control structure

- how to use analytical procedures (the evaluation of financial information in the context of both financial and nonfinancial data)

- auditing accounting estimates

- communication with audit committees

- the auditor's consideration of the company's ability to continue in existence

- the changes in the auditor's report on the financial statements

These last two SASs are particularly important. In the former, or "going concern" statement, the auditor for the first time has a responsibility to alert the reader, by including a paragraph that refers to a footnote(s) in the financial statements, if there is doubt about the company's ability to continue to exist.

But everything eventually depends on the auditor's report, the actual written opinion on the financial statements. This, after all, is the tangible result—and the ostensible purpose—of the audit. As has been noted, the old standard auditor's report contained two paragraphs if everything was all right. The new standard report contains three:

- an introductory paragraph stating that the auditor has audited the financial statements of XYZ Company and that the financial statements are the company's responsibility;

- a scope paragraph explaining the nature of the audit, the nature of the tests conducted, and that the user can take reasonable assurance that the financial statements are free of material misstatement because the audit provides a reasonable basis for the auditor's opinion;

- an opinion paragraph containing the auditor's conclusions

If all is in order, the wording of these three paragraphs is pretty much the same from audit to audit. When things are not in order, additional paragraphs will be added to the report. For example, if there is a departure from GAAP in the financial statements, it must be explained in an extra paragraph. If there are significant, or material, uncertainties about the company's financial statement, additional language is necessary. If there is a going-concern problem, that, too, is explained. If the auditor is unable to obtain sufficient evidence to come to a conclusion, or if there has been a change in accounting methods from a previous year, those will also necessitate additional paragraphs. In short, the reader of financial statements will know immediately that something is wrong or that something has changed if more than the standard three paragraphs appear in the auditor's report.

What does all of this mean for investors? Will it mean that people understand financial statements or the auditor's opinion any better? Will it mean an end to lawsuits against CPA firms if a company fails and people lose money? Is the public's protection any greater now than previously?

In general, the language of the auditor's report is clearer to laymen. Likewise, the responsibilities of the auditor, as opposed to a company's management, are clearly delineated. But people still will not understand the financial statements if they don't read those statements and the footnotes to the statements in conjunction with the auditor's report. And while the auditor's responsibilities are spelled out, there will continue to be lawsuits filed against CPA firms in the wake of business failures because the CPAs are often the only solvent parties left after a business failure.

The public is probably no better protected now than it has been in the past. But that is the public's fault, not the auditor's. Possibly the best protection for the public is in the simple fact that audits take place and are required for publicly traded companies. The very fact that management knows it must submit its financial statements to the audit of an independent certified public accountant in all likelihood is enough to keep the vast majority of managements honest.

The headlines may demand to know where the auditors were. Most of the time they were right there, doing their jobs. In the following chapter, another of Congressman Dingell's questions will be answered: Who audits the auditors?

**An example of an auditor's standard report.**

---

Independent Auditor's Report

To MLJ Company and its Board of Directors:

[*Introductory Paragraph*]

We have audited the accompanying balance sheets of MLJ Company as of December 31, 19X2 and 19X1, and the related statements of income, retained earnings, and cash flows for the years then ended. These financial statements are the responsibility of the Company's management. Our responsibility is to express an opinion on these financial statements based on our audits.

[*Scope Paragraph*]

We conducted our audits in accordance with generally accepted auditing standards. Those standards require that we plan and perform the audit to obtain reasonable assurance about whether the financial statements are free of material misstatement. An audit includes examining, on a test basis, evidence supporting the amounts and disclosures in the financial statements. An audit also includes assessing the accounting principles used and significant estimates made by management, as well as evaluating the overall financial statement presentation. We believe that our audits provide a reasonable basis for our opinion.

[*Opinion Paragraph*]

In our opinion, the financial statements referred to above present fairly, in all material respects, the financial position of MLJ Company as of December 31, 19X2 and 19X1, and the results of its operations and its cash flows for the years then ended in conformity with generally accepted accounting principles.

D. LaRusso & Co.
Certified Public Accountants

February 14, 19X3

**An example of an auditor's qualified opinion.**

---

## Qualified Opinion Because of a Departure From GAAP

*[Emphasis provided for nonstandard wording]*

Independent Auditor's Report

To MLJ Company and its Board of Directors:

We have audited the accompanying balance sheets of MLJ Company as of December 31, 19X2 and 19X1, and the related statements of income, retained earnings, and cash flows for the years then ended. These financial statements are the responsibility of the Company's management. Our responsibility is to express an opinion on these financial statements based on our audits.

We conducted our audits in accordance with generally accepted auditing standards. Those standards require that we plan and perform the audit to obtain reasonable assurance about whether the financial statements are free of material misstatement. An audit includes examining, on a test basis, evidence supporting the amounts and disclosures in the financial statements. An audit also includes assessing the accounting principles used and significant estimates made by management, as well as evaluating the overall financial statement presentation. We believe that our audits provide a reasonable basis for our opinion.

***The Company has excluded, from property and debt in the accompanying balance sheets, certain lease obligations that, in our opinion, should be capitalized in order to conform with generally accepted accounting principles. If these lease obligations were capitalized, property would be increased by $5,000,000 and $5,500,000, long-term debt would be increased by $7,000,000 and $7,200,000, and retained earnings would be decreased by $2,000,000 and $1,700,000 as of December 31, 19X2 and 19X1, respectively. Additionally, net income would be decreased by $650,000 and $500,000 and earnings per share would be decreased by $.65 and $.50, respectively, for the years then ended.***

In our opinion, ***except for the effects of not capitalizing certain lease obligations, as discussed in the preceding paragraph***, the financial statements referred to above present fairly, in all material respects, the financial position of MLJ Company as of December 31, 19X2 and 19X1, and the results of its operations and its cash flows for the years then ended in conformity with generally accepted accounting principles.

D. LaRusso & Co.
Certified Public Accountants

February 14, 19X3

An example of an auditor's adverse opinion.

---

## Adverse Opinion

[*Emphasis provided for nonstandard wording*]

Independent Auditor's Report

To MLJ Company and its Board of Directors:

We have audited the accompanying balance sheets of MLJ Company as of December 31, 19X2 and 19X1, and the related statements of income, retained earnings, and cash flows for the years then ended. These financial statements are the responsibility of the Company's management. Our responsibility is to express an opinion on these financial statements based on our audits.

We conducted our audits in accordance with generally accepted auditing standards. Those standards require that we plan and perform the audit to obtain reasonable assurance about whether the financial statements are free of material misstatement. An audit includes examining, on a test basis, evidence supporting the amounts and disclosures in the financial statements. An audit also includes assessing the accounting principles used and significant estimates made by management, as well as evaluating the overall financial statement presentation. We believe that our audits provide a reasonable basis for our opinion.

***As discussed in Note X to the financial statements, the Company carries its property, plant and equipment accounts at appraisal values, and provides depreciation on the basis of such values. Further, the Company does not provide for income taxes with respect to differences between financial income and taxable income arising because of the use, for income tax purposes, of the installment method of reporting gross profit from certain types of sales. Generally accepted accounting principles require that property, plant and equipment be stated at an amount not in excess of cost, reduced by depreciation based on such amount, and that deferred income taxes be provided.***

***Because of the departures from generally accepted accounting principles identified above, as of December 31, 19X2 and 19X1, inventories have been increased $500,000 and $450,000 by inclusion in manufacturing overhead of depreciation in excess of that based on cost; property, plant and equipment, less accumulated depreciation, is carried at $15,000,000 and $12,500,000 in excess of an amount based on the cost to the Company; and deferred income taxes of $4,000,000 and $2,500,000 have not been recorded; resulting in an increase of $5,000,000 and $2,950,000 in retained earnings and in appraisal surplus of $15,000,000 and $12,500,000, respectively. For the years ended December 31, 19X2 and 19X1, cost of goods sold has been increased $500,000 and $350,000, respectively, because of the effects of the depreciation accounting referred to above and deferred income taxes of $1,500,000 and $1,000,000 have not been provided, resulting in an increase in net income of $1,000,000 and $650,000, respectively.***

***In our opinion, because of the effects of the matters discussed in the preceding paragraphs, the financial statements referred to above do not present fairly***, in conformity with generally accepted accounting principles, the financial position of MLJ Company as of December 31, 19X2 and 19X1, or the results of its operations or its cash flows for the years then ended.

D. LaRusso & Co.

February 14, 19X3 — Certified Public Accountants

# Chapter 7

# HOW ARE ACCOUNTANTS REGULATED?

Despite the fact that accountants are employed by hundreds of thousands of individuals and businesses, there is very little public awareness about how the accounting profession is regulated. This may be so because relatively few complaints are brought against accountants (as compared with the legal and medical professions, for example), or it may be due to the efficiency with which the various layers of regulation actually work. In any event, the profession is closely regulated at four distinct levels: the state, the federal government, congress and the profession itself.

## 1. The State—the Primary Level of Regulation

CPAs, as we have learned, are awarded their certificates and licenses to practice at the state level, by state boards of accountancy. They earn the CPA designation by satisfying educational and experience requirements and by successfully passing the Uniform CPA Examination. They retain it by completing a certain amount of continuing professional education each year. But as the state boards give, so can they take away, and it is only the appropriate state board of accountancy that can revoke a CPA's license to practice.

While the states have the nominal primary authority, in reality they do little more than grant and revoke the license to practice. State boards do enforce rules—backed by legislative statutory authority, in some cases—that pertain to certain things CPAs can or can't do, such as accept commissions, solicit clients or advertise. But the states have relatively little practical authority because they have little investigatory ability. The state boards themselves are most often creations of the state legislature or offshoots of some other regulatory body. In some instances, the same people whose duty it is to regulate accountants must also regulate nurses, chiropractors or librarians. The overall effect is that although the state boards have the power to give and take away a CPA's license, in reality their degree of regulation over the profession is limited.

## 2. The Federal Government

The federal government exercises an even more limited regulatory role in monitoring the accounting profession. It is true that the Securities and Exchange Commission can enforce rules that govern auditors and, to a certain degree, it has regulatory authority over the chief rule-making body, the Financial Accounting Standards Board. But that only affects a limited number of CPAs who happen to be auditors.

In much the same way, the Internal Revenue Service exerts a regulatory authority over those accountants who are tax practitioners. In certain cases—for instance, if a tax preparer knowingly falsifies information—the IRS has the power to bar an accountant from representing a client before the IRS. But other than through the regulations and the guidelines that cover the technical areas of a tax practitioner's work, the IRS has limited meaningful authority over accountants.

## 3. The U.S. Congress

One other arm of the federal government can have considerable authority over accountants: the Congress of the United

States. When Congress exercises that authority, however, it is most often inadvertent. Congress's authority, of course, is vested in its abilities to write the laws of the land, and it is through bills it passes that become laws that it can regulate all the professions, including accounting. Since this authority is grounded in the law, the practical effects of congressional legislation as applied to accountants are usually seen in practice in the nation's courtrooms.

However, Congress can also exact considerable quasi-regulatory influence over the accounting profession via hearings such as those held over the past five years by a number of representatives and senators, most notably Congressman Dingell.

The intense attention on the part of Congress began in 1976 with the preparation of a report prepared by the staff of Senator Lee Metcalf that basically recommended the assumption of strict oversight and regulatory powers by the federal government. Specifically, the Metcalf report supported the notion that auditing standards should be set by a federal agency or by congressional legislation

In the spring of 1977, Senator Metcalf's Senate Subcommittee on Government Operations opened hearings into the regulation of the accounting and auditing rule-making functions of the profession. During the hearings, which lasted more than three months, on and off, the panel heard testimony from the most vociferous critics and the most ardent supporters of the profession. In essence, the subcommittee's recommendations included the formation of an organization made up of large CPA firms that audited publicly traded companies that would undergo mandatory peer reviews of their work. To ensure auditor independence, the firms would be prohibited from doing consulting work for those clients they audited.

The AICPA had more or less anticipated this trend toward government regulation of auditing, particularly the need for a separate regulatory body with power over the auditors of publicly traded companies. Not without dissension, the institute was nevertheless able to bring into existence the Division for CPA Firms, consisting of a section for firms that audited publicly traded companies and another for firms with private company clients. Membership in the Division for CPA Firms was voluntary but included the requirement that the firm's internal quality-control systems undergo peer review at least once every three years. The work of the SEC Practice Section of the Division was monitored by an independent Public Oversight Board that provided oversight of the peer review process and also developed a liaison relationship with the SEC. Having started this movement in 1974, the leaders of the AICPA were able to activate the division shortly after the conclusion of the Metcalf subcommittee hearings in 1977.

Although there are secondary requirements for membership, the key to the regulatory aspects of the Division for CPA Firms is unquestionably the mandatory peer reviews performed on its members. The reviews are done by other independent CPA firms or by CPAs appointed to special peer-review committees.The cost of peer reviews, which can run to several million dollars for the largest firms, are borne by the firms undergoing review. The results of the peer reviews are available to the public upon request from the institute. As noted previously, failure to receive an unqualified (clean) peer review brings remedial rather than punitive sanctions, the rationale being that the ultimate goal of high-quality work can be more readily achieved through education and instruction than through harsher penalties.

The profession's respite from congressional scrutiny was short-lived. In 1985, Congressman John Dingell reopened hearings into regulation of the profession. Dingell, as has been seen, was motivated to a great extent by a series of spectacular business failures that drew the concerted attention of the media. Were the auditors at fault? Congressman Dingell, in attempting to find out, brought about yet more self-examination within the profession and additional change.

The leaders of the AICPA were also better prepared to counter critics this time around. Just prior to the first of the new set of hearings, the AICPA and the four other leading accounting organizations—the American Accounting Association, the Financial Executives Institute, the Internal Auditors

Association and the National Association of Accountants—announced publicly the formation of an independent, private-sector commission to look into the causes of, and ways to prevent, management fraud. Under the leadership of a former SEC commissioner, James C. Treadway, Jr., the National Commission on Fraudulent Financial Reporting spent two years and well over $1 million to investigate and prepare a detailed report on what many felt to be one of the leading causes of business failures—fraud. While the AICPA had formed the commission before Congressman Dingell announced his hearings, the institute's timing was indeed fortuitous.

The final report of the Treadway Commission was issued in October 1987, and was directed at four distinct audiences:

- corporate management
- the accounting profession
- government regulators, including the SEC
- educators

While the report seemed to place the greater share of blame for fraud on the first target, corporate management, the accounting profession came in for its share. Primarily, the Treadway Commission wanted the profession to tighten up auditing standards, ensure that all accounting firms that audited public companies underwent peer review and provide for some public representation on the Auditing Standards Board.

In the two years following the conclusion of the Dingell hearings, the profession continued to tighten up on the regulation of auditors. Accounting firms had always been required to report to the SEC when they ended an engagement as an auditor of a public company (as did the company in its 8-K report, which it must file if it changes auditors or if any other significant change occurs, such as a bankruptcy or takeover). But the company had fifteen days in which to do so, and the auditor had another fifteen after that, plenty of time for the company to declare bankruptcy before investors received any clue that trouble was afoot. Under a new rule for Division for CPA Firm members introduced in 1989, the timing for the auditors to report was shortened to five business days from the day of termination of the engagement.

The SEC requires these reports to eliminate what came to be called "opinion shopping." This can occur when a company doesn't agree with what the auditor says must be included in its financial statements, or when the auditor finds something that must be changed. The company then fires the auditor and goes looking for another that will be more amenable to its accounting. Speeding up the timetable in which the auditor must report to the SEC virtually eliminates any opportunity to engage in opinion shopping.

Finally, in late 1989, the AICPA conducted another ballot of its membership to ask that another new requirement for membership in the AICPA be imposed. The new rule was a requirement that any CPAs who work for firms that audit public companies make sure that their firms belong to the SEC Practice Section of the Division for CPA Firms if they wish to be individual members of the institute, thus ensuring that virtually all such firms undergo peer review. The institute has also provided for public input to the Auditing Standards Board by naming three non-CPAs to its planning committee, the group that determines the subjects the board will consider. This act satisfied all the major recommendations that the Treadway Commission directed toward the profession.

## 4. How Accountants Regulate Themselves

The federal government's greatest influence over the accounting profession affects the most active way in which accountants are regulated—that is, by themselves. It is this self-regulation, which the profession has carried on since its very beginning, that has proved most likely to be the catalyst for congressional hearings and congressional threats to impose, by statute, more direct regulation. To understand best how accountants are regulated, one must look very closely at this process, which also occurs at several distinct levels.

The first level lies in the requirements to join a membership organization, predominantly the American Institute of CPAs.

This group has held the reins of both individual and firm regulation for years and has recently taken steps to bolster its leadership position in the regulatory area and, at the same time, to make that regulation more stringent.

The AICPA's Code of Professional Conduct has existed only since 1973, the year in which a series of pronouncements by an ethics committee was formally codified. Since that time it has been amended several times, most notably in 1977, when CPAs were given the right to solicit clients directly (even clients who were already using another CPA) and to advertise, a right still disputed by many and still prohibited by the Florida Institute of CPAs. The latest and most drastic revision, which created a goal-oriented, more readily enforceable set of rules, occurred in 1988 with the passage of the AICPA membership of the "Plan to Restructure Professional Standards." In 1989, at the insistence of the Federal Trade Commission, the AICPA removed its bans on members' accepting commissions and contingency fee engagements (see Chapter 8).

The Rules of the Code of Professional Conduct are simplicity itself. In brief, they say that:

- AICPA members must be independent and act with integrity and objectivity.

- They must comply with general standards, and those who provide attest services (audits, compilations and reviews) must comply with auditing standards and accounting principles.

- They must protect confidential client information, refrain from acts discreditable to the profession and not advertise in a manner that is false, misleading or deceptive.

- A final rule pertains to the manner in which an accounting firm may be organized and named.

In short, other than the civil and criminal statutes of the states and the federal government, these are the only rules that apply to members of AICPA.

A full-time professional ethics division is responsible for the administration and enforcement of the Code of Professional Conduct. In addition to the constant reexamination and interpretation of these seemingly simple rules, the ethics division staffers also process complaints against individual members or firms that are directed to the AICPA by private persons or that are referred by state CPA societies, state boards of accountancy or agencies of state or federal governments. The ethics division will also initiate investigations when it becomes or is made aware of, a possible act of misconduct through other sources, such as a news story.

In an average year, the division can expect to receive between 600 and 800 such complaints, a majority of them tax-related. A person who feels that he or she has a complaint against a CPA has several means of redress. The matter should first be discussed with the CPA, as many potential conflicts are worked out in this manner, thus avoiding the more formal process of filing a complaint. If mutual discussion fails to solve the problem, the complainant can then file a formal protest with a state CPA society or board of accountancy. Or a complaint can be filed directly with the AICPA, which is where most of these complaints end up anyway, primarily because the AICPA has the means to investigate the complaint and the other bodies do not.

The principal function of the ethics division is to conduct a preliminary investigation of each complaint it receives against an AICPA member. If this investigation determines that there is sufficient evidence to support the complaint, the case is referred to the Joint Trial Board, a series of regional tribunals whose total of thirty-six members are CPAs elected to the position for three-year terms by the institute's governing council. A trial board hears each case referred to it by the Professional Ethics Division and renders its verdict. If found guilty, the member can be directed to undertake additional continuing professional education or be expelled from the AICPA. A member would also be expelled automatically if the institute received word of a conviction for any crime punishable by imprisonment for more than one year, the failure to file an individual income-tax return, the filing of a false income-tax return or aiding in the preparation or presentation of a false income tax return. An individual can also be suspended from AICPA membership for up to two years.

Critics of the profession have maintained that these punishments are meaningless in that loss of membership in the AICPA does not have an effect on the individual's license to practice as a CPA. On the surface this would seem to be a legitimate argument. However, all Trial Board decisions resulting in a guilty verdict are made public by publication in the AICPA's fortnightly "CPA Letter," which goes to all members as well as to a complementary mailing list that includes a number of trade and consumer publications. The institute will also reveal a guilty verdict upon request by the general public. Additionally, the verdicts are monitored closely by the state societies and boards of accountancy, which can, and often do, then take action on their own, sometimes leading to revocation of the license to practice. Finally, membership in the AICPA is considered by the profession to be a hallmark of acceptance. Its loss conveys a stigma that spreads beyond the profession and can ultimately result in a corresponding loss of business.

Should all of the above fail to satisfy someone who has brought a complaint against a CPA, the last recourse is the courts. Many people do, in fact, bring lawsuits against individual CPAs.

## Does Regulation Do Any Good?

There's little doubt that the attention directed toward the accounting profession—by the spectacular failures of some prominent companies and large financial institutions and especially by the periodic Congressional investigations—has resulted in a tightening of already expansive layers of regulation. Perhaps more important, CPAs in public practice who are members of AICPA are subject to periodic peer reviews in order to retain that membership. This is true of all CPAs in public practice, not just auditors. No other profession has as wide-ranging and intensive a system of peer review.

Do these various tiers of regulation and peer review protect the public? In the real world, the burden of protection rides on the party that wishes to be protected. Auditors can and do search for fraud, but auditors are human and may not find it all the time. Auditors report misstatements in financial statements to management, and, if management does not make corrections, the auditors will resign the engagement and report the fact to the SEC. But people may still invest in companies without being aware of any of these warnings. Auditors provide an opinion on whether the figures in financial statements are essentially correct and in accordance with generally accepted accounting principles. They will even say whether a company might have trouble remaining in existence over the course of the months ahead if the evidence warrants such a warning. But auditors are not investment advisers, and they do not give companies a clean bill of health. Essentially, while auditors provide an essential watchdog service, the public is its own best protection against fraud.

# Chapter 8

# ISSUES FOR THE 1990s

Most members of the profession, particularly those in leadership positions in the national membership organizations, undoubtedly felt that the Metcalf hearings of the 1970s and the Dingell hearings of the 1980s were enough conflict to last a lifetime. But a number of other contentious issues combined to bring accountants even more into the spotlight of national media, a position with which they are clearly uncomfortable. The issues described in the following pages promise continued upheaval for the trade.

## Liability Protection

The failures of public companies and financial institutions in the 1980s inevitably generated lawsuits—lawsuits that were usually settled with funds provided by insurance companies under liability protection carried by most accounting firms. As any motorist who has ever had to report an accident to an insurance company knows all too well, the more lawsuits and settlements, the higher the ensuing premiums and the harder to continue sufficient coverage. During 1985 and 1986, that's exactly what happened to accounting firms.

Just as doctors, lawyers and other professionals must carry malpractice insurance, so must accountants. The largest accounting firms have the necessary means to obtain their own insurance. Since the early 1970s, the AICPA has administered an insurance plan for small firms, generally those with up to fifty staff members. At present, that plan provides liability insurance for more than 10,000 firms across the country. Several of the larger state CPA societies also manage insurance programs for firms. Other firms have opted to form pools, find their own insurance or, as the crunch worsened, some chose to practice without any insurance coverage.

As the number of lawsuits against firms mounted, and as the settlements got larger, coverage dwindled to the point where the AICPA plan could provide only $1 million in coverage at almost double the premium, and with higher deductibles. While medical practitioners were complaining the loudest about malpractice insurance coverage, accountants were clearly undergoing an insurance crisis of their own.

In time, the economic climate and pressure against insurance companies in the form of grass-roots legislation, as occurred in California with auto insurance, brought about an improvement in the situation, if not a conclusive end to the crisis. During this period, the AICPA formed its own reinsurance company as a backstop to its regular plan. The company, Amerinst, was financed by member firms that bought shares, and would provide insurance only in the event of another period of unavailability or prohibitively high premiums. Though seemingly in remission now, the liability insurance situation is a problem area that accountants likely have not seen the last of.

# RICO

Wallace Olson, a former president of the AICPA, wrote in his book *The Accounting Profession—Years of Trial 1969–1980:* "The effects of litigation were the root causes of most of the changes that occurred in the profession in the 1970s." As the 1980s drew to a close, the profession was wrestling with the specter of litigation which, if anything, has grown more daunting since Olson wrote about it. One particular type of legislation grew to be a scourge of the profession and brought about the most concerted lobbying effort ever undertaken by the AICPA—RICO, the Racketeer Influenced and Corrupt Organizations Act.

Enacted by a well-intentioned Congress in 1971 to prevent organized crime from penetrating and taking over legitimate businesses, RICO, by the mid-1980s, had come to be seen by many as a law run amok. While many were sued under RICO statutes at both the federal and state levels, accountants, acting in a highly unaccustomed role as political (and public relations) activists, were among the most vociferous interest groups in the fight against the law.

What did they think was so dreadful about RICO? According to the law's critics, who include a number of seemingly incompatible groups in addition to accountants, it isn't necessarily a bad law as long as it is used as Congress intended—that is, against organized crime. Indeed, the law has been used in some notably successful cases to put blatant racketeers out of business. The problem is that the statute has been used in any conceivable situation in which a business dispute has arisen that lends itself to a "pattern of activity," even if that "pattern" consists of using the mail or a telephone as little as twice. The reason for the broadened usage? Losers in a RICO lawsuit can be penalized for triple damages plus costs and attorney's fees. To add insult to injury, they are also branded as "racketeers." To accountants, the latter ignominy is almost as damaging as the monetary penalty.

Accounting firms, in general, do not engage in felonious acts such as murder and extortion. In addition, to lose a RICO lawsuit, the defendant must have a previous conviction of a predicate offense—among those stipulated in the statute are murder, arson, mail fraud and wire fraud. But accounting firms do make considerable use of the mail and telephones, and if it can be shown that they have done so in a pattern—that is, more than once—that has injured a party or been found to have contributed to fraud, then they can be accused of mail fraud or wire fraud. These crimes qualify as predicate offenses under the RICO statutes.

Along with an unlikely group of allies, including the National Association of Manufacturers and the American Federation of Labor-Congress of Industrial Organizations, the accounting profession mounted a determined campaign to pass legislation in Congress to bring the RICO statutes back to their original intent. They've come close. In fact, the House of Representatives in the Ninety-ninth Congress (1986–1987) act-

**The Big Eight in Washington**

One significant change in the accounting profession has come about as the result of a decision on the part of the Big Eight to become more active players in the nation's capital. While the bulk of the accounting profession's government advisory work and lobbying is carried out under the auspices of the AICPA, the major firms have also taken certain initiatives on their own. For example, several firms have hired former congressmen and other government officials and put them in charge of "government relations" departments. Often, prominent partners of these firms have left their companies to take on government jobs, then returned to their firms with the added benefit of having gained well-developed contacts in key federal agencies and an insider's knowledge in general.

ually passed a reform bill, but a companion bill in the Senate went down to a narrow defeat on the last day of the congressional session.

The AICPA was forced into opposing a reform bill under consideration in the Senate during the One-hundredth Congress because the bill contained a provision that exempted "small investors" from the reform. Under the bill's definition, almost anyone could qualify as a small investor and thus continue to be eligible to sue accounting firms under RICO. The profession is hopeful that the end of the use of the RICO statutes against accounting firms will soon be legislated.

## Joint and Several Liability, and Privity

Unfortunately, the removal of RICO would not completely ease the profession's worries about litigation. In many states, the legal concept of joint and several liability is still very much in effect. Under joint and several liability, a defendant can be held liable for 100 percent of the damages in a liability case even though his actual responsibility might be as low as 1 percent. Apply this menacing concept to the "deep pocket" syndrome and you have a CPA firm's nightmare. As you will recall, an auditor is very often the only solvent party in the aftermath of a business failure. Investors or creditors who have lost money because of the failure look around for some party to sue, and the only viable target is the accounting firm. Under joint and several liability, if the firm is found to be negligent in its audit, or in some other service it provided for the failed company, it may be forced to pay up to 100 percent of the plaintiff's monetary loss.

At the same time, the profession is supporting the concept of privity, under which a third party may not sue unless there has been a contractual relationship with the plaintiff. Privity is followed only in several states, and the profession seeks to foster it nationwide.

Taken together, these problems have led the profession to call for reform of some aspects of the legal system. Several years ago, a special committee on accountants' legal liability was formed, and it spearheaded the lobbying effort to change the system. At the same time, the AICPA has filed *amicus curiae* (friend of the court) briefs in cases in which the joint and several liability and privity issues have been contested. While there have been victories in several states, possibly the most significant milestone in the battle to reform the tort system was the introduction in June 1989 of a bill in the U.S. Senate to eliminate the joint and several concept. The profession's legal problems, though, will most likely continue to be an issue for at least the immediate future.

## The Savings and Loan Crisis

When a crisis occurs that has even the slightest financial overtones or implications, sooner or later an accounting firm is going to be sued. That has proved to be the case frequently enough in the last twenty years that it comes as no surprise to the profession when it does happen. But even the most resigned were taken aback when several parties, most of whom bore far more responsibility for causing the crisis than did accountants, tried to place the blame for the savings and loan crisis of 1988-1989 on CPAs.

The causes of the thrift crisis were several, though fairly obvious:

- unacceptably poor management of the thrifts after deregulation of the industry, which permitted loans to risky ventures that subsequently failed

- lax regulation by Congress and federal regulators who, in addition to committing other lapses, permitted the thrifts to use looser accounting methods than GAAP

- a severe downturn in the economy in the Southwest, which

saw massive failures in the real estate and energy industries, both heavy borrowers from the thrifts

There is little doubt that greed and fraud on the part of the thrift owners and managers also played a strong role in creating the mess.

When it was finally recognized, shortly after the Bush Administration took office, that the state of affairs was truly a disaster, the inevitable happened—congressional committees held hearings. Their questions were familiar ones for the CPAs called to testify: Where were the auditors? Why didn't they provide warnings that this calamity was about to happen?

Adding to the profession's dilemma, the General Accounting Office, the chief investigative body of Congress, issued a report just as the hearings were getting under way that cited a study of the audits of twenty-nine thrifts in the southwest and found that eleven of these audits had been substandard. Then the Federal Home Loan Bank Board, the parent body of the Federal Savings and Loan Insurance Corporation, announced that it was suing eleven accounting firms for faulty audits.

With all of this going on, it was no great surprise when the chairman of the House Banking Committee announced that CPAs were to blame for the thrift crisis. As *The New York Times* of March 12, 1989, put it: "This, of course, is not the first time that the accounting profession has come under fire in the wake of a financial collapse. . . . But never before have accountants faced anything as brutal, or as potentially costly, as this onslaught."

Once again the profession's leaders based their defense on overall statistics that showed only a tiny fraction of all audits to be faulty. The GAO study did not show a true picture, they said, because it examined only a handful of thrift audits. Had it examined all of them, it would have found the same small percentage of poor audits as in the case of publicly traded companies. The profession could also document warnings it had sent to Congress against deregulation of the thrift industry and strident cries against letting them use less-stringent accounting methods. "Alarm bells were sounded by the profession in the early 1980s," testified AICPA President Philip B. Chenok, "and they have gone largely unattended."

The accountants' defense was relatively successful. Although the occasional story appeared in the media blaming the CPAs for a specific failure, criticism by the Congressmen and the GAO largely died away, especially after the AICPA promised to provide a quick update of its audit guide for savings-and-loan associations. The FDIC lawsuits have yet to be tried, but the firms involved have maintained consistently that they provided good audits—audits that in fact disclosed the problems that eventually broke the thrifts—but say that the warnings contained in the audits were simply ignored.

* * *

As the 1980s drew to a close, the accounting profession faced a number of other issues, but none of them seemed to have the potential for such great financial liability and public-image damage as those just described. There are changes coming in accounting curricula, as the profession prepares to implement the 150-hour requirement. The fact must be faced that even though some 140,000 candidates are sitting for the Uniform CPA Examination in 1989, fewer students are graduating with accounting degrees. Competition from other financially related industries, such as investment banking, has caused concern, and educators within the profession are addressing this issue as well.

There is increasing competition for clients among the larger firms as corporations merge or take one another over. Each time this happens, an accounting firm loses an audit client. Little wonder, then, that the firms are turning more and more to consulting engagements as the growth in revenue from tax and audit work diminishes. The more this happens, the more closely those who regulate the profession, such as the SEC, will look at the potential for conflict of interest and loss of independence. We have already seen instances of big firms completely reorganizing to accommodate consulting partners. In the future, it is likely that many of these consulting partners may not even be certified public accountants, which will bring about a reexamination of the rules concerning who can be a partner in a CPA firm.

# Chapter 9

# THE ACCOUNTANT AND TAXES

Lots of accountants do nothing but tax work. Without a doubt, of all the accountant stereotypes, that of the accountant as tax professional is by far the most common. According to industry statistics, of all those who make their livings in the tax field, there are more accountants than any other type, including tax attorneys, enrolled agents, tax paraprofessionals, moonlighters and other part-time tax preparers.

Accountants work in all areas of taxes. They prepare tax returns for people in all economic brackets and for businesses of all sizes. Tax professionals range from those who work during tax season for tax-preparation chains such as H & R Block to partners of the largest accounting firms with the most prestigious corporate clients. Others, who may or may not call themselves accountants, may work out of storefronts or their own garages, and also prepare a significant number of the more than 100 million 1988 tax returns the IRS received that were prepared by someone other than the taxpayer. A majority of the approximately 40,000 sole practitioner members of the AICPA, practicing for the most part in towns and smaller cities across the country, concentrate on tax work with individuals and small businesses.

Literally thousands of CPAs, working for medium-size and large accounting firms, handle the tax planning and advisory work for almost all of the country's businesses, from the smallest entrepreneurial venture to IBM and General Motors. Indeed, the tax staffs of any one of the larger CPA firms are far larger than entire law firms. Without the tax expertise of accountants, the voluntary tax system—unlike any other in the world in its dependence on basic human honesty—simply wouldn't be possible.

Working in the tax field can take several forms, the most usual of which is tax preparation and advice, the reason most individuals hire an accountant. More farsighted individuals consult tax practitioners well before it's time to prepare the tax return. Tax planning, more and more a part of what has come to be termed "personal financial planning" (see Chapter 10), now consumes a more substantial part of the tax practitioner's time, as the actual number crunching, or putting the data on the tax forms and making the necessary calculations, is more commonly done by computer. Not only does this work make it easier to prepare the eventual and inevitable tax return as April approaches, but it more importantly positions the taxpayer to take the fullest advantage of the tax laws. With the Tax Reform Act of 1986, planning ahead is very much the name of the game.

## How Does One Know If One Needs an Accountant?

This is the most common question many people ask as tax season approaches. Except for the obvious—the very wealthy with incredibly complicated financial situations, the stubborn individualists who absolutely refuse to tackle tax forms, or the many who simply can't understand them—asking if you need an accountant's help during tax season is a supremely legitimate question. The key to the answer is the complexity of the individual taxpayer's financial situation.

If there is only one source of income—generally, wages paid by an employer—the taxpayer should be able to handle the chore without professional help. Many people in this situation benefit from the relatively new Form 1040 EZ that the Internal Revenue Service put into use in 1983.

While an audit by the IRS may be the most feared government intrusion into an individual's life, it is usually not that complicated or stressful provided the taxpayer can provide the documentation to substantiate his or her case. Audits come about most often when a computer has noticed a "red flag" on a taxpayer's return, generally an itemized deduction or other statement that is well above the average for the taxpayer's income level. These "red flags" could include, for instance, unusually high medical or charitable deductions or a dubious miscellaneous deduction. The tax returns of self-employed persons receive special scrutiny, especially when a deduction is taken for an office in the home. In other words, anything on the return that does not fall within an accepted average for a certain income level, or is in any way out of the ordinary, is likely to spark the IRS's interest, although, it should be made clear, it may not necessarily lead to an audit.

What should the taxpayer do if the dreaded notice does turn up? An excellent first step is to consult with the professional who prepared the tax return, or, if no such tax preparer was used, visit a CPA. The tax preparer should be able, and the CPA almost certainly should be able, to judge whether the item under question by the IRS is defendable. If so, collect all supporting documents—you

For most people, the situation is a bit more complicated but not yet too complex. They may have some income from interest and dividends, and, as is becoming more and more common, there may be a second wage earner in the household. These taxpayers should still be able to prepare their own returns by carefully following the instructions on the tax forms and perhaps making use of one of the commercial tax guides found in most bookstores. But some of these folks simply

---

should always save and organize all paperwork, such as receipts, that has anything to do with your tax preparation—and visit the IRS agent and carefully explain your position. Your CPA can accompany you on the audit and can even represent you under the provisions of the Taxpayers' Bill of Rights.

If it turns out that there is not enough detailed supportive evidence for the position taken, particularly when cash receipts are needed to document business deductions for travel and entertainment, the chances are that the IRS agent will disallow the deduction and the taxpayer will be hit with a penalty and interest. Whatever the case, the taxpayer should always visit the IRS agent, explain the position and the reasons why it was taken. In some cases, and particularly if there are no other questionable items on the return, the agent may accept the explanation and allow the deduction.

The taxpayer has further recourse when the IRS agent refuses to accept a position. A request can be made to speak with the agent's manager. More likely would be the procedure whereby the taxpayer would file an appeal for an administrative hearing. The last recourse is the tax court, where the taxpayer would be represented by a tax attorney or a CPA who has been accepted to practice before the court.

---

don't want to bother, and they are a large part of the more than 100 million who will decide to hire a professional tax preparer to do the job for them.

To whom should these taxpayers turn? From a cost-effective standpoint, people in this situation should not consider going to a CPA (or a tax attorney or enrolled agent, for that matter). The chain tax-preparation services such as H & R Block are capable and efficient in these cases, although the quality of their work would not match a CPA firm on a consistent basis. By making use of part-time accountants, accounting students or free-lancers with an aptitude for taxes, these businesses prepare literally millions of returns, accurately and at quite reasonable prices every year. In fact, *Money* magazine annually distributes a hypothetical tax return to a range of tax practitioners and asks them to complete it. Each year, return preparers from the chains compete on an equal footing with CPAs and tax attorneys. While this is hardly a scientific litmus test, it does demonstrate that the chains possess a definite expertise.

As we've learned, though, in about half the states, anyone can call himself or herself an accountant. When it comes to taxes, absolutely anyone can call himself or herself a tax preparer, even if he or she never prepared one previously. In the case of tax preparation, then, it is strictly *caveat emptor.* All that means is when you hear about the guy down the block who's doing tax returns in his garage during tax season, and charging a fire-sale rate, be cautious. Consider whether you would want this type of tax preparer to handle some of your most important financial transactions.

Deciding when you need help on your tax return is not in any way governed by the amount of your income. As people move up the income ladder, though, their financial status does tend to become more complex. These people are the borderline cases who might be perfectly capable of doing their own returns but who could probably benefit from going to a CPA or enrolled agent. They will have income from several sources: investment income from securities, perhaps rent from a vacation house, income (or losses) from a hobby at which they work in addition to their regular job. The result of these different incomes is that they necessitate using more than just the usual IRS tax forms. Additionally, they will also be affected by changes in the tax laws and, while there isn't a major tax bill such as the Tax Reform Act of 1986 coming out of Congress every year, the tax laws do change almost every year. These people will most likely benefit from the expertise of a CPA tax practitioner.

## What Does a Tax Accountant Cost?

Almost all CPAs charge hourly fees for tax work, and these fees can vary widely depending on a number of factors. An urban firm is likely to have a higher hourly rate than would a rural firm. Rates might also vary in different parts of the country. The most important determining factor, aside from how long it takes to do the actual work, is the individual in the firm who is doing the work. The senior tax partner will command a higher hourly rate than a staff accountant. In essence, the firm will match the complexity of the return with the appropriate level of expertise; the client, therefore, is paying for the level of expertise needed. Whether or not the firm sends the returns out to a computer service center for the actual number crunching could also affect the final pricetag, although more and more firms are developing their own in-house computer capability.

Dollarwise, the charge for preparing a relatively uncomplicated return might run around $300. Charges escalate rapidly, and it is not uncommon for even modestly wealthy people to pay a bill between $2,000 and $4,000, which is why it is extremely important to try to estimate the cost-effectiveness of going to a tax professional. The cost is balanced, of course, by the presumption that the taxpayer is getting the most accurate return and, hopefully, the best possible refund. The large national firms generally don't do much individual tax preparation, except for the executives of their corporate clients, the very wealthy and celebrities. But tax work is decidedly a very big part of many of the good-sized regional firms and is probably the predominant type of work done by most small accounting firms and sole practitioners.

## How Does One Find an Accountant?

Accountants also do almost all of the tax-preparation work for the thousands of small businesses that make up the industrial and service backbone of the nation's economy. This is an area that the larger accounting firms are exploring, making inroads into what had been the sole province of the local and regional firms. Business owners don't often have to ask themselves whether or not they need an accountant's tax help—they know they do. But they regularly have to ask how to find an accountant. The answer is to ask for references, and the best people to ask are other professionals who either deal with accountants themselves or whose clients deal with accountants. Bankers, lawyers, securities brokers and insurance agents are good choices. But the best reference for a business owner is a competitor who is in the same line of business. If that person is happy with his or her accountant, the client's search is probably over.

Armed with four or five references, the prospective client must then get out and do some interviewing, face to face, almost always in the accountant's office. The first obvious question is: What kind of experience does the accountant (and the firm) have in the searcher's line of business? References should be secured and checked, and it should be determined, insofar as possible, who in the firm will be the contact and who will be doing the bulk of the work. When the decision is made to hire a firm, the client should ask for an engagement letter, which spells out exactly what the accountant will be providing in the way of services and, usually, approximately how much it will cost. This can head off a host of unpleasant surprises that could crop up down the road.

## When the IRS Comes Calling

CPA tax practitioners have one other vital function that they perform for both individual and business taxpayers. They can represent clients before the IRS (and some are also certified to practice before the tax court) in case of a tax audit. The tax audit, a taxpayer's worst nightmare, is probably one of the most feared phenomena that the government can inflict upon its citizenry, even though less than 2 percent of individual taxpayers get called in any one year (see box on pages 76-77). But the CPA can relieve much of the pressure and anxiety if a client is one of the unlucky ones who gets audited. The CPA can even represent the taxpayer at the preliminary meetings with the local IRS agent, thanks mainly to the Taxpayers' Bill of Rights, passed in 1988.

## If You're Dissatisfied

What if the taxpayer doesn't like the job the tax preparer did? The CPA, of course, is subject to several tiers of regulation, and the tax professional is also guided by the AICPA's Statements of Responsibilities in Tax Practice. The IRS regulations for tax practitioners, of course, have the force of law. As noted, a majority of the complaints received by the AICPA's professional ethics division are tax related. Many are unfounded, the most common being that the preparer didn't get a big enough refund for the client. (If a tax preparer promises a refund ahead of time, you'd best look elsewhere for help.)

Concerning penalties (and interest) imposed by the IRS for a mistake or a late filing, they are the taxpayer's responsibility. The tax preparer has no obligation to pay these penalties even if the fault lies with him or her, although the IRS can inflict monetary penalties on preparers who make flagrant mistakes. The taxpayer also has recourse as noted in the chapter on regulation of the profession.

# Rewriting the Tax Laws

If tax planning and tax preparation—for individuals and businesses alike—are the mainstays of the tax practitioner's work, there is another element of tax work that goes on largely behind the scenes, and almost exclusively in Washington, D.C. Many people think of the Internal Revenue Code as a relatively stable entity, disturbed occasionally by a major tax law such as the Tax Reform Act of 1986, which attempted to simplify and make equitable the way people and businesses were taxed. What they don't realize is that the tax code is constantly changing as the IRS and the Treasury Department issue regulations, interpretations and guidelines on almost every aspect of the body of the law. It is in this never quiet arena that the members of various tax-related organizations, especially the committees of the Tax Division of the AICPA, the Tax Section of the American Bar Association, the Tax Executives Institute and a number of other groups, are hard at work advising, counseling and sometimes lobbying those who create and administer the tax laws.

This is accomplished in a number of ways. When the tax-writing committees of Congress are considering tax legislation, as they do most of the time during which Congress is in session, the CPAs provide input on who will be affected by proposed changes, and, more important, how they will be affected. It is a sad but true fact that many of the effects of often well-intentioned tax legislation are unforeseen and blatantly unfair to some unsuspecting special-interest group. This kind of give and take often results in a confrontational relationship with the Ways and Means Committee of the House of Representatives, the Senate Finance Committee and the staff of the Joint Congressional Tax Committee, the group that takes the House's and the Senate's different versions of the same bill and reconciles them into one law that can be presented to the President.

The accounting profession's accomplishments in this behind-the-scenes work go largely unnoticed. But there are some notable successes, such as the Taxpayers' Bill of Rights, passed by Congress in 1988 after strenuous grass-roots lobbying by accountants, primarily in state CPA societies around the country. CPAs were also responsible for enabling many small businesses to remain on a fiscal-year schedule for tax purposes when it seemed that the tax laws would force them to change to a calendar year. Had this happened, it would have caused great inconvenience for industries whose busy seasons did not coincide with the calendar.

This extremely important advisory work is carried out by CPAs from large and small firms, from sole practitioners to the largest international organizations, who voluntarily join one of the twenty-seven committees and subcommittees and fifteen special task forces of the AICPA Tax Division. These groups focus on an incredible variety of topics, from tax forms to employee benefit plans, tax accounting to computers in tax work, tax legislation to corporate or international taxation. Of course, they devote hundreds of hours to studying the greater issues such as tax complexity. The committees of the Tax Division receive vital assistance from the Tax Division staff working out of the AICPA's Washington office. These individuals spend as much time in the Treasury Department, the Internal Revenue Service and on Capitol Hill as they do in their own offices, and they are often called upon to help prepare testimony to be given before the tax-writing committees of Congress.

The relationship between the accounting profession and the Treasury Department, of which the Internal Revenue Service is a subsidiary organization, is a mutually respectful one. Indeed, *USA Today,* announcing the appointment of new IRS Commissioner Fred Goldberg in May 1989, said that Goldberg ". . . would have a tough act to follow. The AICPA wanted to make Larry Gibbs [Goldberg's predecessor] IRS commissioner for life," presumably because Gibbs listened to and respected the accountants' counsel. The ultimate beneficiary of this relationship is the taxpayer.

It is becoming apparent that the chances of more major

changes being made in the tax code are highly likely. By June 1989, AICPA representatives had already testified at least a dozen times before congressional committees on subjects as diverse as leveraged buyouts, alternative minimum tax calculation for corporations, employee benefits and civil tax penalties. The administration was calling for reduced capital-gains taxes and no additional tax increases. During and after the changes leading up to TRA '86, the AICPA had continually called for a moratorium on tax-law change. It was tax-writing business as usual in Washington.

In the meantime, accountants are doing what they can to make changes that make sense and to help the individual and business taxpayer come through the uncertainty and complexity in the best possible shape. Both the AICPA and the ABA have had committees on tax simplification in place for over a year. There is great hope that kinder, gentler and simpler tax laws for all taxpayers will soon be in effect.

# Chapter 10

# PERSONAL FINANCIAL PLANNING

During the mid-1980s, business publications and stories in the business sections of newspapers began referring to a "new industry." They called it personal financial planning and applied it to a whole range of practitioners in various professions and industries: investment advisers, securities dealers, lawyers, insurance and real estate salesmen, and, almost as an afterthought, accountants. Almost overnight, there appeared classes and seminars for personal financial planners. Two different organizations, the International Association of Financial Planning and the College of Financial Planning, engaged in a not always friendly rivalry to promote and, to a limited degree, provide a general certification for these new professionals.

Certified public accountants were somewhat surprised by all the fuss being paid to financial planners. They thought that they had been doing financial planning for quite a while—since the inception of the federal income tax, as a matter of fact. Indeed, when the government levied a personal income tax, it implicitly challenged taxpayers to come up with ways to protect their money, and so created a whole nation of financial planners. Not surprisingly, many of them needed help, and the logical choice to turn to for tax help was CPAs. Thinking a year ahead at a time had come to be a normal habit in tax planning. Thinking several years ahead or more became retirement planning, and so on until CPAs and other tax practitioners were actually performing, well, personal financial planning, as it has come to be known today.

The sudden appearance of this "new" industry stemmed primarily from the unprecedented growth in complexity in the area of both business and personal finance. Taxes hadn't become more complex. In the same manner, estate planning, risk management, personal investing, with all new manner of financial instruments to play with, was even more complicated. One could even invest while covering insurance needs, as insurance companies marketed policies keyed to the stock markets. Banks got into the life-insurance business, savings and loans were investing in real estate—everyone had a new gimmick and a strong desire to plan their clients' finances in all areas.

With the growing number of personal financial planners and their various accreditations as "certified financial planner" (or some similar title), it wasn't long before the accounting profession, particularly the smaller firms whose members had been engaged in providing financial advice for a long time, came to realize that they were in danger of losing a number of their clients. In response, many CPAs registered with the IAFP. Taking a more active role, the Colorado Society of CPAs put into place its own accreditation program, the first acknowledgment by any part of the accounting profession of a specialty area. The Colorado program subsequently became the basis for the AICPA personal financial planning specialty and was also the impetus for the institute's examination of a range of potential specialty areas.

If CPAs are now very much in competition with all manner of other personal financial planners, there remains one vivid difference in the equation: how they charge for their services. Traditionally, CPAs, almost without exception, have charged their clients an hourly fee. The rules of conduct of the AICPA prohibit its members from accepting commissions or contingency fees (except in certain carefully defined tax engagements). The underlying rationale for this position was that only through avoiding commissions could the practitioner maintain independence and objectivity, which he or she was bound to do by the AICPA bylaws. The practical effect of the rule was to prevent CPAs from selling financial or investment instruments such as stocks, bonds, securities, life insurance or real estate, or to take referral fees for sending clients to vendors of those products.

In January 1985, the Federal Trade Commission of the United States, which periodically examines the rules governing the practice of different professions, initiated a study of the AICPA's rules. The FTC made no secret of the fact that the outcome of its investigation would find the institute's ban on commissions and contingency fees anti-competitive and in restraint of trade. In fact, that's exactly what happened. In 1987, the FTC sent the AICPA a consent agreement by which the AICPA would immediately drop its bans and permit its members to take commissions and contingency fees. In a rare display of unanimity, the board of directors of the institute voted to refuse the FTC request.

While the FTC appeared adamant in its quest to do away with the bans, it at least seemed to be willing to consider the profession's arguments on independence and objectivity, in the areas of attest services (audits, compilations and reviews). In 1988 a second consent agreement arrived at the institute, requiring the AICPA to remove the ban on CPAs taking commissions from clients, except for those clients for which they were already providing attest services. A CPA would also have to disclose to a client the fact that he or she would receive a commission for the work performed. The ban on contingency fees would be removed. At a special meeting of the AICPA council in August 1988, AICPA leaders signed the agreement. As of this writing, the FTC has yet to complete its final review.

The agreement applies only to members of the AICPA, who, admittedly, include most of those CPAs who engage in personal financial planning. As members of the AICPA, they would be free to accept commissions and take contingency-fee engagements. Or would they? All CPAs, in addition to holding their national membership, are licensed by a state board of accountancy, and most also belong to a state CPA society. As of late 1989, only five state boards of accountancy—Maryland, Oklahoma, Texas, South Dakota and West Virginia—permit CPAs to take commissions, and at least one of those, Texas, is seriously considering introducing a law in the state legislature that would rescind this permission.

On the flip side of the coin, several other states have introduced legislation that would statutorily prohibit the acceptance of commissions by accountants. The FTC is seriously lobbying these states to drop the proposed bans, but there is some question as to what authority the FTC has over a legislative statute at the state level. A highly vocal and active CPA has threatened to take states to court to overturn the prohibitions, but as of this date the states seem adamant in their refusal to relax the bans. After all the commotion, nothing seems to have changed very much.

All this negotiation and legal maneuvering have taken place largely over the heads of the practitioners, but some business writers have tried to explore how they feel about the issue and what they would do if all the bans are ultimately removed. A strong majority of CPA financial planners have indicated that they would not, in any case, accept commissions, but would continue to charge clients on a fee-only basis. A few have said that they would monitor the market closely, and if it appeared that they were losing business to competitors who took commissions, they would strongly consider doing the same. A decided minority said they would take immediate advantage of the freedom to accept commissions.

The position of the FTC is well known. By removing the ban, clients who go to CPAs for personal financial services would have the opportunity to meet all their needs in one place, thus giving them access to a more open market through opening up competition. Other professionals who currently provide those services through the sale of financial instruments, investment methods, real estate and life insurance are adamantly against the notion of CPAs getting into the market for these products. As we have seen, the accountants don't particularly want to sell products since they maintain that the sale of a product is likely to prejudice the objective advice that the CPA provides to the client.

Interestingly, no one seems to have asked the general public what it prefers, although the Lou Harris poll done for the AICPA in 1986 did indicate that a knowledgeable public believed that the accounting profession's strong selling points were its independence and objectivity. Doubtless, the issue of commissions will be with us for a while longer. But it is highly unlikely that one will ever witness many CPAs selling life insurance or real estate.

Regardless of what develops in the manner of services that accountants will offer in their personal financial planning practices, it is almost certain that they will remain in competition with financial planners from other industries and professions. And, since all of these various participants in the financial planning game work under different rules, there will continue to be conflict over how the "new" industry should be regulated. Part of the problem is that the various bodies that might provide overall regulation have been unable to arrive at a mutually satisfactory definition of the term "financial planning." It is obvious that not all financial planners are investment advisers, and it is equally obvious that those who call themselves investment advisers would be unqualified to render more than basic tax consultation. At present, some heated battles are taking place in state legislatures over this matter.

Currently, anyone can become an investment adviser (or, for that matter, a financial planner), merely by paying a $150 fee to register with the Securities and Exchange Commission. Non-accountant investment advisers, however, want anyone who offers investment advice to be regulated by someone, either at the state or federal level. Advocates of this position, the accountants say, fail to see any distinction between those who merely offer advice and those who actually sell investment products. Those who sell stocks, bonds and securities, of course, must be registered with the National Association of Securities Dealers. In June 1989, a regulatory bill passed by both houses of the Maryland legislature was vetoed by the governor at the urging of lobbyists for investment advisers because the bill covered all financial planners except certified public accountants. At about the same time, the SEC voted to suggest that Congress consider writing legislation that would create a self-regulatory body, similar to the NASD, to regulate financial planners. This would require testing and licensing.

Accountants, on the other hand, claim that they are already subject to testing and stringent licensing requirements at the state level and must also obey the rules of their respective state boards of accountancy and membership organizations. In the case of those who belong to the AICPA, that means undergoing peer review. The accountants also cite the existence of a federal statute, the Investment Advisers Act of 1940, and securities laws in most states which, they claim, are adequate protection against fraud and other potential abuses. The CPAs also point out that most documented abuse found in this area has been connected with the sale of products, an activity in which most accountants have little or no interest.

While the accounting profession will likely continue to oppose any regulation of financial planners that includes CPAs, it is also taking distinct steps toward ensuring that its members are positioned to take their fair share of the market. In fact, the goal of the AICPA's Personal Financial Planning Division is to have that growing number of potential clients for these services think of CPAs when they need help, much the same as they do when the subject is taxes. To accomplish this, the division is encouraging firms of all sizes to get involved with financial planning and is providing a whole series of practice development materials, practice management aids and other guidelines to help them along the way. The result of all this activity will undoubtedly be a greater CPA presence in the financial planning arena in years to come.

# Chapter 11

# THE FUTURE OF THE ACCOUNTING PROFESSION

Changes in the accounting profession have occurred at a dizzying pace in the past ten years, and this is likely to be the case for at least the near future. In fact, most knowledgeable observers of the profession think it will change even more rapidly.

While the supply of graduates may be on an ever so slightly downward trend, the demand for new accountants, and also the competition for their services, will increase. Increased demand will likely mean higher starting salaries for new CPAs. This in turn will lead to increased costs for accounting firms, which are more than likely to be passed on to clients in the form of higher fees. All of this, of course, depends on the clients' recognizing the value of the services provided by the accounting firms and continuing to be willing to pay for those services, which they almost certainly will.

A vital part of the changing equation will be the new services that clients will continue to demand from public accounting firms and the new assignments that employers will assign to their CPA employees. It is difficult to predict with any precision what these new jobs will be, but regardless of their nature, they will demand both broader general talents and more specialized abilities on the part of those doing the work. This will require the schools of business to educate accounting majors in areas that may turn out to be significantly different from today's.

- Computer skills

As the computers used in business themselves become increasingly sophisticated, so will the students have to become more computer-intelligent to keep up.

- Ethics

There will probably be a continuing emphasis placed on teaching business ethics, as there seems little evidence pointing to a decline in white-collar crime.

- Business law

It would not be a great shock to see accounting students taking more in-depth courses in business law. The last several years have seen increased ethical lapses in the business community. This, combined with the fact that CPAs are becoming involved in more and more aspects of business in general, means that CPAs must be schooled in the legal ramifications of the services and advice they offer.

- Economics

As we approach the year 1992 and immediately thereafter, there will be a great deal of concentration placed on world economics, international trade and global finance. That year, the world will see the dropping of trade barriers in Western Europe and the adoption of a single currency for those nations. This is considered by many experts to be one of the most dramatic and significant economic events since the first

Industrial Revolution. International accounting firms are already turning their planning in that direction. Several have looked beyond 1992 to the day when even the Eastern European countries may become integrated into this dynamic economic sphere, and, in anticipation, they have already opened offices in the Soviet Union and Hungary. The ever-growing economic might of Asia will also have great influence on the overall global picture. Increased concentration will be placed on the study of national accounting standards in an attempt to arrive at a generally harmonized set of international standards, a task that is already in motion under the guidance of the International Federation of Accountants. This will not be easy to achieve. In fact, it would not be surprising to see a whole new breed of internationalist accountant, with a world view, rather than a national view of the profession emerging from these changes.

**The Big 5?**

At press time, mergers among the Big 8 had created what might now be called the Big 5. Here's how they rank, based on 1988 revenues:

| | 1988 U.S. Revenue (millions) | 1988 Worldwide Revenue (millions) |
|---|---|---|
| Arthur Andersen/ Price Waterhouse | $2,670 | $5,020 |
| Ernst & Young | $2,017 | $4,244 |
| KPMG (Peat Marwick) | $1,639 | $3,900 |
| Deloitte & Touche | $1,616 | $3,760 |
| Coopers & Lybrand | $1,141 | $2,495 |

Source: *Bowman's Accounting Report*

# What of the Big Eight?

With a major merger between Peat Marwick and KMG Main Hurdman in 1986, and the even bigger merger of Ernst & Whinney and Arthur Young in 1989, many think there will be even further consolidation of the largest firms, perhaps to the point where there will be a Big Four or Five.

Present circumstances would seem to support this view. Competition is already strong for audit clients. Each firm has different regional and industrial strengths. When a good fit between two firms is possible, it creates a much stronger and more competitive firm. In fact, it may now be that the great size of the two new firms created from the mergers, Ernst & Young and KMG Peat Marwick, along with Arthur Andersen, previously the largest firm, have made inevitable further mergers of the rest of the Big Eight with one another or with the bigger "second tier" firms. Jim Emerson, the editor of *The Big Eight Review* (which will now, presumably, have to come up with a new title), says, "I believe any firm which desires to be in a future leadership position rivaling their previous 'Big Eight' status must make their move now . . . . Whether further consolidation occurs this month or in two years, the KPMG, AA and E&Y positions ensures more will take place."

The biggest firms, and very likely most other medium- to large-size firms, as well, will certainly be concentrating increasingly on consulting work as the percentage of their revenue growth derived from auditing and accounting work continues to decline. The "second tier" firm BDO Seidman has formed a subsidiary investment firm that has registered with the SEC as a securities dealer. The consulting partners in the other large firms, who have historically played second fiddle to the audit and tax partners, could follow the lead of the maverick Arthur Andersen partners who left the accounting firm to form their own consulting firm if they do not achieve equal status and equal pay.

Competition will also come from outside the profession from the aforementioned consulting firms. Large and small firms alike will have to devote more time to marketing, and this will result in increased expenditures on advertising and public-relations activities. Further activity by the Federal Trade Commission may result in changes in the names of CPA firms, which have historically been named after founding or contemporary partners. The FTC, however, may insist that accounting firms be permitted to call themselves anything they wish.

These changes will have equal impact on the smaller firms. CPAs who work for these firms feel that they, too, are facing a challenging but potentially rewarding future if they can cope with five specific areas of change. According to Charles Kaiser, chairman of Pannell Kerr Forster, these are:

- changing technology
- increasing complexity of rules and regulations
- competition
- the need to employ more non-CPAs
- the general shortage of graduates

Still, the smaller firms have historically served small business and, while there is now stiff competition from the larger firms even in this area, there is no sign that the number of small businesses are diminishing. The small firms that will succeed are those that are well managed. Management techniques and the art of practice management will be two more areas of expertise that CPA partners will have to master.

We have already witnessed the dawn of the age of specialization in the accounting profession, and specialization will become ever more apparent in the next decade. The AICPA has already designated one specialty area—personal financial planning—and is actively considering many others under the three general headings of accounting and auditing, federal taxation and management advisory services.

Possible specialties under accounting and auditing include:

- dealerships (cars, trucks, boats, farming equipment)
- government
- health-care institutions
- insurance
- non-profit organizations
- regulated transportation
- utilities

Potential tax specialties are:

- corporate
- estate, gift and fiduciary
- exempt organizations
- individual
- international
- partnership

Management advisory service specialties include:

- business computing
- financial analysis and planning
- information technology
- operations consulting
- bankruptcies

## The Computer Age

If one were to pick just a single area that will both cause the most change and yet dominate the future of the accounting profession, it would have to be computers. The dawning of the computer age has already caused astounding changes in the profession. Yet the changes already made will seem as nothing by the turn of the century. It is highly unlikely that any single area of the profession will be unaffected by the advances made in computer technology. The AICPA has already introduced five computer software programs that have greatly simplified the paper work auditors and accountants must create in the course of their work. The larger CPA firms and independent producers are very much involved in the marketing of software. Many non-accountants use commercial tax-preparation software, as do almost all accounting firms, at least to do the number crunching.

## The Outlook for Women

Yes, the accounting profession will still depend on people, and more and more of those people will be women. In 1988, fifty-two percent of the accounting graduates and just about half of those passing the Uniform CPA Examination were women, according to the AICPA and NASBA. While their numbers are still relatively small as far as being partners in the larger firms are concerned, they will gradually achieve better representation in this area as well. But the mere number of women will not automatically erase the last vestiges of male dominance of the profession. While there is still much work to be done in this regard, there is decided movement. The larger accounting firms of the 1990s will not only have more women partners and professionals, but they will also have those women's babies—not working, but playing in child-care centers operated by the firms. Women will be working more often on flexible work schedules that will permit them to pursue a career and a family simultaneously.

## An Eye on the Capitol

Finally, the profession will be forced to keep in close contact with goings-on in Washington, D.C., where the nation's lawmakers will periodically find some catalyst—probably in the form of a business failure or scandal in a particular industry—that will cause them to focus their attention on the quality of the work done by CPAs. There will be congressional hearings, undoubtedly, and the concomitant regrouping by the profession's leadership, but that will most likely be all. While accountants seem to be able to excite great skepticism in congressmen every ten years or so, they also seem able to convince them that no amount of additional government regulation would cause the profession to perform any better. In fact, it might do just the opposite. One reason our elected representatives don't push it any further is that, by and large, the people who use the profession's services are pretty well satisfied with the job accountants do.

# GLOSSARY

**accredited personal financial specialist (APFS):** a specialty designation awarded through testing by the AICPA to CPAs who are personal financial planners

**American Institute of Certified Public Accountants (AICPA):** the national professional association of CPAs in the United States

**audit:** an examination of a company's accounting records and internal controls, including an opinion by the auditor, required by the SEC for all publicly traded companies; also, an examination of a taxpayer's return by the IRS when the service has a question or disagrees with a position taken by the taxpayer

**Auditing Standards Board (ABS):** a senior technical committee of the AICPA responsible for setting generally accepted auditing standards

**Big Eight:** designation applied to the eight largest public accounting firms; has been reduced by several industry mergers

**bookkeeping:** classifying and recording a business's transactions in an orderly way, usually adhering to specific rules of bookkeeping

**certified public accountant (CPA):** an individual who has passed the Uniform CPA Examination and met certain education and experience requirements and has received a license from a state board of accountancy

**compilation:** the presentation, in the form of financial statements, of information about a company that is the representation of the company's management; no assurance of conformity to GAAP

**contingency fee:** a payment for services that is dependent on an amount received as a result of those services

**cost accounting:** analyzing and reporting on current or predicted costs

**division for CPA firms:** a membership division of the AICPA for firms; conducts peer review of member firms

**Federal Trade Commission (FTC):** the U.S. government agency responsible for the organization and conduct of business in the United States

**Financial Accounting Standards Board (FASB):** the independent private-sector organization that establishes accounting principles in the United States

**financial statements:** the balance sheet, income statement and other documentation of financial information prepared by a company; the body of information subject to an audit

**fiscal year:** an arbitrary period of twelve consecutive months chosen by a business as the accounting period for annual reports

**generally accepted accounting principles (GAAP):** the rules and guidelines for financial accounting

**generally accepted auditing standards (GAAS):** the rule by which an independent auditor conducts an external audit of a business enterprise

**going concern:** a business that is expected to survive in business in the future

**internal audit:** an examination of a company by its own employees to determine whether internal control procedures are effective

**Internal Revenue Code:** the tax laws of the United States

**Internal Revenue Service (IRS):** a subsidiary agency of the U.S. Department of the Treasury that administers the tax laws and collects and examines individual and business tax returns

**opinion:** the judgment by the independent auditor of whether a company's financial statements conform with GAAP

**peer review:** the examination of an accounting firm's operating practices and internal controls, and particularly its accounting and auditing work, by an independent peer review team of CPAs

**private companies practice section:** one of two sections of the AICPA's Division for CPA Firms, for firms that have private companies as clients

**public oversight board:** an independent oversight group that monitors the operation of the Division for CPA Firms

**qualified opinion:** a part of the auditor's report that points out a limitation or uncertainty in or about an item in a company's financial statements

**quality review:** the examination of a CPA firm's practices by another group of CPAs; similar to peer review

**review:** a report on a company's financial statements by an independent CPA; gives lesser assurance than an audit that the financial statements are in conformity with GAAP

**Securities and Exchange Commission (SEC):** the U.S. agency that monitors the financial reporting of publicly traded companies and that has ultimate authority over CPAs who audit those companies

**sole practitioner:** an individual who practices alone as a CPA

**unqualified opinion:** a standard auditor's report that a company's financial statements conform with GAAP

# SUGGESTED READING

## BOOKS

*The Accounting Profession—Years of Trial 1969-1980*
Wallace E. Olson. The American Institute of CPAs, New York, NY, 1982

*The Accounting Wars*
Mark Stevens. Macmillan Publishing Co., New York, NY, 1985

*The Rise of the Accounting Profession (Two Volumes)*
John L. Carey. The American Institute of CPAs, New York, NY, 1970

## PERIODICALS

*Accounting Today*
Published bi-weekly by Lebhar-Friedman, New York, NY

*Bowman's Accounting Report*
Published monthly by Hudson-Sayer Professional Services Marketing, Inc., Atlanta, GA

*CPA Journal*
Published monthly by the New York State Society of CPAs, New York, NY

*Journal of Accountancy*
Published monthly by the American Institute of CPAs, New York, NY

*New Accountant*
Published bi-monthly by New Duboif Corporation, Glen Cove, NY

*Practical Accountant*
Published monthly by Warren, Gorham & Lamont, New York, NY

# INDEX